I am my dear E

yours affy

A. Clarke

THE

Triumphs of Industry;

ILLUSTRATED BY THE

LIFE

OF

ADAM CLARKE, LL.D.

"Industry, order, and early rising, will enable a man to go through a great deal of work."

"You remember, my dear lad, my motto is—BE DILIGENT, LOSE NO TIME." *Dr. Adam Clarke's Letter to his Son.*

Philadelphia:
AMERICAN SUNDAY-SCHOOL UNION,
No. 316 CHESTNUT STREET.
NEW YORK: No. 147 NASSAU ST......*BOSTON:* No. 9 CORNHILL.
LOUISVILLE: No. 103 FOURTH ST.

☞ *No books are published by the* AMERICAN SUNDAY-SCHOOL UNION *without the sanction of the Committee of Publication, consisting of fourteen members, from the following denominations of Christians, viz. Baptist, Methodist, Congregational, Episcopal, Presbyterian, Lutheran, and Reformed Dutch. Not more than three of the members can be of the same denomination, and no book can be published to which any member of the Committee shall object.*

PREFACE.

The material from which this volume has been written was obtained from "The Memoirs of Adam Clarke," by himself and a member of his family; "Everett's Adam Clarke Portrayed;" "Everett's Wesleyan Takings;" "The Life of Mrs. Adam Clarke;" "Dunn's Life of Adam Clarke;" "West's Sketches of Wesleyan Preachers;" various articles in the "Wesleyan Methodist Magazines," and numerous sermons in the possession of the writer, preached on the occasion of Dr. Clarke's death, by co-labourers and friends. The author has also consulted "Grindrod's Laws and Regulations of Wesleyan Methodism," for a knowledge of that peculiar church economy with which Dr. Clarke was so intimately connected, and has given to the readers the advantage of the facts obtained from it, to enable them better to understand the biography.

His greatest indebtedness is to the "Memoirs," "The Portraiture," and "Mrs. Clarke's Life"—and about equally to the first two. Mr. Everett was, for twenty years, one of Dr. Clarke's confidential friends; and his manuscript was revised, he informs us, by one of Dr. Clarke's daughters. He writes with the warmth of personal friendship, and the evident integrity of the Christian historian.

While we have thus spared no pains in collecting all the facts which have been printed in England that would throw light upon the character of the eminent commentator,—a valuable part of which has never before been published in this country,—we have endeavoured to present them in a manner adapted to the youth of the United States. We hope the freedom of style, in the use of illustrations, will not render the work less acceptable to adult readers.

CONTENTS.

CHAPTER I.

EARLY PHYSICAL AND MENTAL TRAITS.

CHAPTER II.

EARLY MORAL AND RELIGIOUS TRAINING.

CHAPTER III.

THE GREAT CHANGE.

CHAPTER IV.

THE IMMEDIATE FRUIT OF THE GREAT CHANGE.

CHAPTER V.

PROVIDENTIAL GUIDANCE TO THE MINISTRY.

CHAPTER VI.

THE MINISTRY COMMENCED.

CHAPTER VII.

TOILS, PRIVATIONS, AND SUCCESS.

CHAPTER XI.

THE PULPIT AND THE FAMILY.

CHAPTER XII.

UNSOUGHT HONOURS.

CHAPTER XIII.

THE COMPLETION OF THE COMMENTARY, AND CLOSE OF LABOUR FOR THE RECORD COMMISSION.

CHAPTER XIV.

LABOURS MORE ABUNDANT.

CHAPTER XV.

RETIRED, BUT NOT RESTING.

CHAPTER XVI.

THE PALACE OF THE GREAT, AND THE COTTAGE OF THE POOR.

CHAPTER XVII.

AN APPROPRIATE, LAST LABOUR.

CHAPTER XVIII.

A MORE FAMILIAR ACQUAINTANCE.

CHAPTER XIX.

THE CLOSING SCENE.

LIFE OF ADAM CLARKE.

CHAPTER I.

EARLY PHYSICAL AND MENTAL TRAITS.

Adam Clarke's birth-place—His father and mother. *Early Physical Traits*—Original endowments—Taught to work at an early age—An early riser—Fondness for fishing. *Mental Characteristics*—An incident of the school-room—His first school-house—His library—His strong desire for knowledge.

ADAM CLARKE was born in Ireland, near the waters of the North Channel, in the county of Londonderry, and in the obscure village of Maybeg. It is remarkable that his parents differed in their recollection of the year of his birth, his father thinking that he was born in 1762, and his mother believing it to have been in 1760; and this last there is every reason to conclude is the true date.

The ruins of the stone house in which he was born remained in his manhood. It was situated on the side of a well-cultivated hill. "The open plain at the foot of the hill, the mountains on each side in the distance, and the river winding its way between them," were

2

very picturesque to the mind of the youth, and were spoken of by him in later years with great vivacity.

His father descended from a good family, and was well educated, having graduated at the Glasgow University with honour, and was considered a superior scholar. Being disappointed of attaining a place in the ministry of the established church, he adopted the laborious occupation of a teacher, which he pursued through life.

The mother of Adam Clarke was of Scotch descent. Her son says, "she was not a beauty, but she was a sensible woman—rather above the average height—had an air of peculiar gracefulness in her movements—appearing rather to glide along than to walk, and was as straight in her old age as in her prime."

There was one son, Tracy, older than Adam, who became somewhat distinguished as a surgeon in the English navy,—and three daughters.

The father of Adam Clarke seems to have been a man of genuine piety, but not sympathetic in his nature, and a stern disciplinarian. He had high notions of the authority of the parent and teacher. He did not so much persuade as command.

His mother was not less pious, nor had she a lower standard of parental government, but with her strictness she used some devices to secure obedience to her rules.

But before looking at the moral training of the son in the hands of his parents, let us examine his natural traits as exhibited in childhood. The formation of the character is, under God, the work of education. The capacity of the mind is God's gift, who distributes the measure with wonderful diversity and in infinite wisdom. A knowledge of his original endowments is absolutely necessary, in judging how far any man may be a fair example to others. We shall endeavour to put the reader in possession, to the extent of our materials, of this knowledge. As we are now speaking of a child, it will suit well the present period of the narrative to refer to him by his Christian name.

Adam had, in childhood, excellent health. He inherited a good constitution. God gave him a sound body, and he took as much care of it as was possible, consistently with hard study and incessant labour. He began to walk at the age of eight months, and a month later ran in the field near the house after his father. As he was not a petted child, he learned habits of hardihood at this tender age.

As he advanced in years, he manifested a love for manly exercises. These developed the bodily strength. But from an early age he did not need sport of any kind as exercise. The circumstances of his father, who was dependent upon his daily labour for the means of maintaining his family, required the help of his sons on a small farm, on which he laboured in the intervals of the school-hours.

From the first, Adam loved to work. He remarked, on one occasion in after life, "There has not been a day since I was eight years of age, in which I have not done something to get my bread. I have known nothing but labour from my boyhood; the bread of idleness was never eaten by me. At seven years of age my father sent me out to watch the cows; soon after that, I was ordered to the mountains to help to shear the sheep. At twelve, I held the plough in a field near my father's house, which we farmed; and, as a proof that I was not over and above strong, the ploughshare coming into contact with a stone which lay under the surface of the earth, threw me up between the shafts which I had been holding with firm grasp, and sent me with violence among the horses' feet. Little as my hand was, I could take it full of wheat, and, with the sheet wrapped around me, could scatter the seed over the soil,—yes, and have as good and regular crops, too, as any of my neighbours. I was probably made hard, and to use my limbs at an early period, that my body might strengthen by exercise; for I had need of all the strength and fortitude I possessed."

Few men have accomplished much in life, who have wasted the early hours of the day in sleep. A fixed habit of early rising, so as to become a part of a man's daily experience through life, must be formed in youth. The father of Adam called his family from their beds at four o'clock in summer, and long before daylight in winter, and gave each his portion of labour with which to commence the day. But his father was too well acquainted with the nature of the youthful mind to require incessant toil. Such amusements were allowed as were not injurious to the mind, and might benefit the health.

Adam was very fond of fishing. Standing, when an old man, on a rock projecting into the sea, not far from the residence of his boyhood, he exclaimed, "On this rock, when a boy, I used to fish. There," pointing to a hollow in the rock, "I beat the shell-fish, and taking up the pounded substance, fish and shell, I went farther down, sowed it like seed upon the water, deliberately walking up again, when shoals of fish were accustomed to follow: then I had nothing to do but take my lines and draw them out. Here, too, I was once bathing, and, coming out of the water, I fell back, and cut my leg in different places, the scars of which I carry with me to this day."

At eight years of age, when many children, not afterward distinguished, show great quickness in learning, Adam's mind was inactive in reference to books. From whatever cause, he could not, for a time, keep up with his school-fellows. As soon as he could read tolerably well, his father put a Latin grammar into his hands, requiring him to commit it to memory.

The recitations dragged heavily. His father sternly demanded perfect lessons. Other boys of his age committed page after page of the grammar; but Adam at last threw down the book in despair, and took his place with an English class. When he appeared on the floor to recite, his father demanded, in a tone that he remembered in old age, "Sir, what brought you here? Where is your Latin grammar?" In a piteous tone he answered, "I cannot learn it." The reproof which followed, and the command to resume his task, sent Adam, trembling, to his seat.

Just before this circumstance occurred, a teacher of a neighbouring village was visiting the school, and heard his father's censure upon Adam's dulness. The stranger, laying his hand kindly upon the boy's head, said, soothingly, "Oh, he will make a fine scholar yet!" These words made a deep impression in this hour of trouble. But a more powerful stimulant drove his mind fairly from its resting-place. As he sat down and resumed his Latin grammar, a class-mate called him a stupid fellow, and began rattling it over, to show how *he* could say it, and ran on, with page after page, which looked (to poor Adam) like a month's task.

But the spirit of the boy was roused. "What," said he, "am I to be the butt of ridicule for all my class-mates? Am I to be the dunce of the school!"

The difficulty was gone, "as if," to use his own words, "something had broken within him." In a short time the lesson which seemed unconquerable was recited without an omission. Page followed page, much faster than his teacher wished to hear him recite. From that time Adam out-studied and out-learned every boy in school.

Very soon after this memorable period, some friends of Mr. Clarke, while loitering in the grave-yard adjoining the school-room, were puzzling over a Latin epitaph on a tombstone. "You are wrong in your rendering,—both of you," said Mr. Clarke, who stood near. "I will call my Addy, and he will do better." Adam came, and, first looking carefully, (for he knew the consequences of a blunder,) read it correctly: "Fortune favours the courageous."

From the period above mentioned, Adam manifested a strong passion for books and for study. A desire to pry into every thing was a marked trait of his mind. When he was about eight years of age, his father, having moved to Grove, ten miles from his former residence, Adam commenced in earnest to work on the farm as well as in the study. The little school-house, in which the foundation of his education was laid, was situated on the skirt of a wood, on a gently rising eminence, behind which a hill, thickly covered with trees and bushes, rose to a considerable height. Before it was a beautiful landscape of streams and cultivated fields and grazing flocks. Here he read the Eclogues and Georgics of Virgil, with a keen appreciation of the rural scenes they describe. His brother Tracy and himself studied in the school and worked on the farm a day in turn, and what was learned in the school by one was carefully rehearsed by the other, so that but little of the lessons was lost, while a hearty relish was kept up for that which was learned.

His library at this time was peculiar, and shows his mental inclination. It was obtained by saving economically every penny earned in various little services to others. A great favourite among his books was Robinson Crusoe. This he seems to have received as sober history, until his father rather damped his interest in it by saying it was written in a government prison. Books of Eastern stories were among his choice ones, and from them he thought he received his first promptings to the study of Eastern literature,—particularly that of the Holy Land and Arabia, for which he afterwards became so distinguished. Pilgrim's Progress was numbered among those he read with intense interest. Many of the old English ballads were treasured up and read over and over. Various histories and biographies were also on the list.

A brief notice of the habits of the Irish peasantry, by whom he was surrounded, will show the source of much of his taste for tales and ballads. During the long winter evenings, the people of a neighbourhood assembled in turns at each other's cottages. While the females were employed in spinning, the young men in weaving and the children in some simple work, the old people rehearsed stories of the warlike deeds of their ancestors, or a tale of the imagination, handed down, perhaps, from father to son, for many generations. A supper of the most simple food was then served, and the whole closed by plays and feats of strength among the young people, while the aged were delighted spectators. Though Adam might not be often a participator in these scenes, they had their influence, as the little stream helps to swell the river.

His early efforts in composition were rather remarkable; one of which, in rhyme, composed when he was nine years of age, shows that he had gathered a large number of items from classical fables. The one referred to exhibits no remarkable *poetic* talents, but much cheerfulness of spirit.

His desire to obtain a knowledge of every thing about him was shown in various ways. He gazed at the stars, and longed to know their names and places in the heavens. He obtained an old spy-glass, and with this, often without hat and bare-legged, he sallied out, on a clear frosty night, to make observations on the moon and stars. He studied the signs of the weather, until he thought himself somewhat "weather-wise." The ultimate fruit of this early observation was one of his first published articles, called "A Fair and Foul Weather Prognosticator." "Many times," he says, "I have, even in tender youth, watched the heavens with anxiety, examined the different appearances of the morning and evening sun, the phases of the moon, the scintillations of the stars, the course and colour of the clouds, the flight of the crow and the swallow, the gambols of the colt, the fluttering of the ducks, and the loud screams of the sea-mews—not forgetting even the hue and croaking of the frogs," these various objects being supposed to furnish indications, more or less reliable, of changes in the weather.

CHAPTER II.

EARLY MORAL AND RELIGIOUS TRAINING.

Morning and evening prayers—Anecdote of J. Q. Adams—The parental discipline—An incident of his early conviction—A little companion—The conversation—Deep feeling—The different view of his feelings by his father and mother—Adam Clarke's subsequent opinion of early religious convictions.

It is proper to state that Adam's father was a member of the Episcopal Church. He was exact in his observance of its religious services; a firm believer in its doctrines, and constant at its communion.

His mother, was a Presbyterian, and attended the ministry and sacraments of her own church. The children usually went with their father. The mother taught them the catechism of each communion. The following is a part of the morning and evening prayers, in verse, which they learned from her:—

Evening Prayer.

I go to bed as to my grave,
I pray to God my life to save,
But if I die before I wake,
I pray to God my soul to take.

Morning Prayer.

Preserve me, Lord, amid the crowd,
From every thought that's vain and proud;
And raise my wandering mind to see
How good it is to trust in thee!

The late John Quincy Adams is said to have remarked, in the latter part of his life, that the evening prayer beginning,

"Now I lay me down to sleep,"

which is the more common form of the one given above, was taught him in infancy by his mother, and he had never once, up to old age, retired to rest at night without repeating it! If such men as Adam Clarke and John Q. Adams loved, as they did, these simple prayers, let no youth be ashamed to repeat them, nor any parent be ashamed to teach them.

Adam's mother made a constant use of the Bible in her religious instructions. If he had done wrong, he was often admonished by some appropriate quotation from the Scriptures, conveying the desired reproof; and so great was the reverence that she instilled into his mind for that holy book, that if he had it in his hand for the purpose of reading it, and was disposed to whistle a tune or to be merry, he would do neither until the book was laid aside. Her instructions left in his mind a profound reverence for God, amounting almost to terror in view of his awful justice. The doctrine of the new birth was clearly recognised and taught by this excellent woman. The religious training of her children was what is sometimes called *Puritanical;* and, doubtless, was very much like that so strongly enforced at the same period by the Puritan fathers of New England.

Obedience was a word her son well understood. But her requirements were so judiciously mingled with instruction and persuasion, that to her, under God, more than to all other causes, her son owned his future goodness. His father, toiling to obtain even small pecuniary resources, in school from eleven to fourteen hours a day, and several hours each day on the farm, seems to have left to her, mostly, the religious care of the children; yet, accompanying him to public worship, and kneeling with him at the family altar, they doubtless were impressed by his paternal example and genuine piety.

The early effect of these influences, through God's Spirit, may be seen in the following incident. It will indirectly illustrate the truth of the above remarks.

Adam, when about six years of age, had a little associate, with whom he was one day walking in the field, hand in hand. They sat down on a bank, and began to enter into very serious conversation. They both became much affected, and this was deepened to exquisite distress, by the following observations made by his associate, little Brooks: "Oh, Addy, Addy," said he, "what a dreadful thing is eternity! And oh, how dreadful to be put into hell-fire, and to be burned there forever and ever!" They both wept bitterly, and, as they could, begged God to forgive their sins; and they made to each other strong promises of amendment. They wept until they were really exhausted, and departed from each other with full and pensive hearts.

In reviewing this circumstance, Adam has been heard to say, "I was then truly and deeply convinced that I was a sinner, and that I was liable to eternal punishment; and that nothing but the mercy of God could save me from it—though I was not so conscious of any other sin as that of disobedience to my parents, which at that time affected me most forcibly. When I left my little companion I went home; told the whole matter to my mother, with a full heart, expressing a hope that I should never more say any bad words, or refuse to do what she or father might command. She was both surprised and affected; gave me much encouragement, and prayed heartily for me. With a glad heart she communicated the information to my father, on whom I could see it did not make the same impression—for he had little opinion of pious resolutions in childish minds, though he feared God, and was a serious, conscientious man. I must own, that the way in which he treated it was very discouraging to my mind, and served to mingle impressions with my serious feelings which were not friendly to their permanence: yet the impression, though it grew faint, did not wear away. It was laid deep in the consideration of eternity, and my accountableness to God for my conduct, and the absolute necessity of enjoying his favour, that I might never taste the bitter pains of eternal death. Had I had any person to point out 'the Lamb of God, which taketh away the sins of the world,' I believe I should then have been found as capable of repentance and faith—my youth and circumstances considered—as I ever was afterward."

CHAPTER III.

THE GREAT CHANGE.

Removes to Ballyaherton—The house in which he spent his boyhood—The "Old Church"—The "New Church"—Impressive incidents—The lost knife—A deception—Providential escapes—The "False Lights"—Apparent drowning—A scene on the North Channel—A novel preacher—Conviction for sin—Diligence in business—A temporary error—The crisis—The change.

THE period of Adam Clarke's life upon which we dwell in this chapter, including the time of THE GREAT CHANGE, which he experienced through Divine grace, extends from about his tenth to his eighteenth year, and brings us forward to 1778.

Near the commencement of this period his father removed to Ballyaherton, a parish of Agherton, and still nearer than before to the shore of the North Channel. The house which the family occupied is seen in the accompanying picture, accurately exhibiting it as it was at this time, excepting its now newly thatched roof. It had the appearance of three huts joined together. The rooms were all on the ground floor. There was a garden attached to

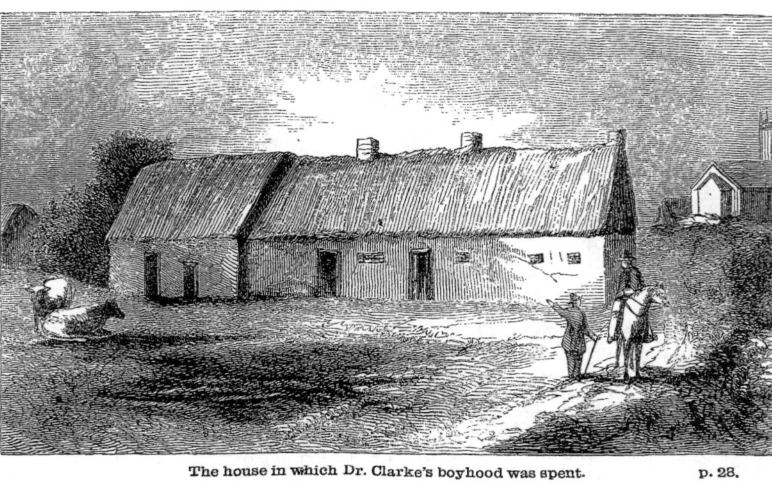

The house in which Dr. Clarke's boyhood was spent. p. 23.

it. Not far distant were the residences of the two lords of the soil, Mr. Cromie and Counsellor O'Neill. With one of the sons of the latter, Adam formed quite an intimacy, which was recollected with pleasure by both in mature years.

It will be perceived that the dwelling is sufficiently unpretending in its character, and is an impressive intimation of the worldly circumstances of Mr. Clarke. It, however, does not so much indicate the position in society of its occupant as it would in New England or the Middle States, where, land being cheap, people of very small property may own a dwelling of some pretensions to elegance.

The hedge on the right is a much more common enclosure in Ireland than in this country. The whole has an air of quiet and contentment well calculated to make a favourable impression on the mind of a boy of ten years of age.

Now we are looking at pictures, the reader will please to turn to the representation of the "old church." (P. 162.) This is from the drawing of the ruins, as they appeared when it was visited by Dr. Clarke, near the close of his life, and was sketched by a friend who accompanied him. He remarked at the time of this visit, "It was within the walls of that ruin that I proceeded with my *hic, hæc, hoc;* and it was within that sacred enclosure also that I first received the

Lord's Supper. Mr. Smith was the officiating clergyman; he preached in the church on the Sunday; and my father used it as a school-house during the week. There were only two pews in it, one on each side of the pulpit, both of them very large—one for Mr. Cromie's family, and one for Counsellor O'Neill's, the latter of which stood a little forward. The other part of the ground-floor was occupied with moveable seats." The friend who accompanied the doctor, not perceiving any provision for a fire, and for the escape of the smoke, made a remark to that effect. "We had a fire on the middle of the floor," he replied, "around which we sat in winter; and the building being large, and the roof high, the smoke had sufficient room to fly about without rendering those on the floor invisible to each other." The interior arrangement, as above described, will remind some of our readers of the early churches of New England, a few of which have been seen, in their dilapidation, by the present generation. We think, however, the fire in the centre cannot be equalled by the reminiscences of *our* "oldest times."

"There is no man," says an elegant writer, "who has not some interesting associations with particular scenes, and who does not feel their sublimity and beauty enhanced by such connection. The view of the house where one was born, of the school where one was educated, and where the gay years of infancy were passed, is indifferent to no man."

A few incidents of Adam's life at this period will show how easily his mind was affected by comparatively trivial circumstances, which became, in their combined influence, of much importance in shaping his future character. The following were taken down from the lips of Dr. Clarke by a friend; and the improvement that was made of them, when they occurred, shows the early fruit of a well-cultivated conscience.

"When I was at school," the Doctor said, "I lost a knife, and deplored it to a friend of mine, who appeared to sympathize with me. 'I wish I had known that yesterday, Addy,' said he, 'for I had a nice one with two blades, and an ivory handle, studded with silver, which I would have given you.' After working upon my feelings for some time, and thus heightening the disappointment, he at length dashed all my hopes by telling me he had no such thing. I felt so much on the occasion that I resolved, from that moment, never to tell any person what he had lost by what he might have possessed,—supposing the provision might have been forthcoming." Thus he drew, at once, good from the wrong-doing of others, and the disappointments of his own mind.

Another incident from the same source shows how deeply seated in his mind were his mother's instructions, to regard always the exact truth. It will be remembered that the impression made by these incidents had gone down with Adam to old age, and were called up in the course of social conversation.

"I was but a little fellow," said he. "A boy had some new farthings given to him; he called me to him, and, looking downward at the time, said, 'Addy, Addy, I have lost my farthings; help me to seek for them.' I sought, and sought anxiously, almost every spire of grass, for several yards around. But neither of us could find them. On giving up all for lost, I accidentally looked at his hand as he was raising himself from the ground, and found the coins had been locked in it, the whole of the time, by the three fingers, while he was pointing with the forefinger and thumb of the same hand, and scraping the grass and soil with them." He adds, in substance, that the disappointed feeling experienced was trifling, he having had no personal interest in the search, in comparison with the pain he felt at the falsehood employed to effect the deception. This left the circumstance engraven upon his mind.

In studying the means which God uses to bring men to a saving knowledge of the truth, we should pay special attention to his providences. They are often the occasions through which the Spirit applies the revealed word, and by them he wisely revives and deepens impressions made by other means. It was thus that he dealt with young Clarke. We select the following illustrations of this statement, from among several others, because he was heard often to refer to them, especially the second one, as having made a deep impression on his own mind. It is not so much the circumstance, as the use we are able to make of it, or the workings of the Spirit through it, which renders it interesting in contemplating the formation of character.

"When I was a boy about ten years of age," said the Doctor, while retracing the scenes of his youth, "my mother sent me one evening to the house of a friend. A bog had to be crossed, a full mile in length; a dense mist spread itself around, and enclosed me in its depths, long before I had reached the end of the journey. Unable to see a step of the way, and in great perplexity, one of the lights, to which you have alluded, (an *ignis fatuus,*) suddenly sprang up before me. It was the first I had ever seen, though I had often heard of them; and the frightful stories connected with them were brought to my recollection, with tenfold force, by the reality then presented to view. When I drew backward, it followed—moving to the right or left, it moved also in the same direction; on stepping forward, it likewise advanced. All around was a mere bog, without any regular track, and consequently every step was threatened with danger, and any one might have proved fatal to life. I stood and trembled; and yet to have remained without further effort was to fix myself there till morning. I resolved at length to grope my way cautiously out, though utterly at a loss in what direction to move, having changed my position so often already, in consequence of the *ignis fatuus.** After hazarding a few steps I heard a rustling noise; the sound of my foot had alarmed some wild ducks, which frequented the place; and knowing some of their haunts, it instantly occurred to me to listen in what direction they flew, and to follow the sound, as I concluded they would take the direction of the water which adjoined the place to which I was going. Accordingly, lending an anxiously attentive ear, and following on, I was brought, in consequence of this attention to their flight, within a few yards of the friend's door to whom I was sent."

The thankful mind of Adam, instructed as he was to feel that God is ever near, and that "in him we live, and move, and have our being," referred this escape, by means so unexpected and so simple, to the hand of his Heavenly Father.

---

* We need scarcely tell even our young readers that there is nothing frightful in the *ignis fatuus.* It is sometimes called *Jack-o'-the-lantern,* or *Will-with-a-wisp.* It is a gas, which arises probably from decaying matter in damp places, and the light which it emits is like that which we have seen thrown out from pieces of rotten wood--called a *phosphoretic light.* The reason that it follows, or goes from, a person near it, is this: the motion of the body disturbs the air, and makes a current, which, when the person approaches, drives the very light, shining gas away, and, on his receding, draws it toward him.

Port Stuart. p. 35.

On another occasion Dr. Clarke was visiting the sea-shore near Port-Stuart, not far from the place of his father's former residence just described, and called upon a friend whose house embraced a view of the Irish Channel. In the course of a social conversation, glancing his eye out at the end window, along the sand, he remarked, "One of the most remarkable providences connected with my life befell me on a spot which I have just in view." He then proceeded to give the following narrative of the event:—"I came down to the shore yonder, riding on a mare of my father's, determined to have a swim. Firmly seated, we proceeded until we were beyond the breakers; but when we had got over swell after swell, and were proceeding still onward to the ocean, the mare and myself were swamped in a moment! I, of course, lost my seat, and fell into the water. All my views and ideas seemed instantly and entirely changed; and I had sensations of the most perfect felicity that it is possible, independent of rapture, for the human mind to feel. I had no pain from the moment I was submerged; a kind of general representation, nearly of green colour, became visible to me, in which a multitude of objects were seen, not one of which, however, bore the least analogy to any thing I had ever seen before. How long I continued in this state He only knows who saved my life; but one wave after another—for the tide was then coming in

—rolled me to the shore. The first sensation, on coming to life again, was as if a spear had been run through my heart; this I felt on getting the first draught of fresh air, when the lungs were inflated, occasioned merely by the pressure of the atmosphere. After a short time had elapsed, I was capable of sitting up; the intense pain at my heart, however, continued; but I had felt no pain from the moment I was submerged, till the time when my head was brought above water, and the air once more entered my lungs. Upon looking round for the mare, I found she had proceeded a considerable distance on her way home."

The reader will see, in the plate, the house in which this narrative was given, and the beach where Adam was so wonderfully preserved from drowning.

These providences preceded the time when he sought to give his heart to God, and were, through the Holy Spirit, helping to prepare it to yield to Him who was calling him in these acts of his preserving power.

Adam was at this time about seventeen years of age; was upright in his outward deportment, and esteemed, with good reason, a young man of excellent character. But God, who knoweth the heart, saw that his affections were not set upon Him. While he feared and reverenced God, he did not love him like one "born of the Spirit." He lacked one thing. This he knew, and, at times, felt deeply. He had been taught that he was to be saved from sin by faith in Christ; but the great doctrine of the atonement was not clearly taught by the ministers under whose preaching he at this time sat. At this critical period, Mark O'Neill, his constant play-fellow, said to him one day, "Let us go to Burnside. A very singular kind of preacher, called a Methodist, is to preach there. We shall have fine sport." Adam's mind at once shrank from the idea of going to a religious meeting of any kind for amusement, and this he declared to his companion, at the same time consenting to go.

This decided and frank avowal of his feelings, at the risk of provoking the ridicule of his companions, was, perhaps, the turning point in his religious character. The distance was not great. They found the people assembled in a barn. Soon the preacher appeared. He was to Adam a singular-looking man. He was plain and serious, but so different in dress from any clergyman he had ever seen, that the mind of his curious hearer was deeply impressed. His words were earnest and practical. After the preaching, Adam with many others, followed him into the house belonging to the owner of the barn, where he again spoke to the people about their spiritual interests.

The effect of the words of this stranger upon young Clarke's mind was not very decided. He continued to hear with interest these itinerant preachers, for some time. They were "the helpers," (as he styled them,) of Mr. Wesley, the founder of Methodism. They were men of small attainments in learning, but often of marked natural abilities, generally deeply pious and extremely self-sacrificing.

Adam was especially benefited by Mr. Thomas Barber, one of these "helpers." His preaching was accompanied by the power of God's Spirit to his heart. He now felt, as he had not been accustomed to feel, that he was a sinner. But it was not a sudden and overwhelming feeling in his case. The Spirit works with different manifestations in different persons. In Adam there was a steadily increasing sense of guilt before God. He now began to read the Bible, as he had never read it before, *in course*, and attentively, studying to ascertain God's will concerning his duty. He prayed much, that God would enlighten his mind by his Spirit. If he came to a passage which he did not understand, he would immediately fall upon his knees, and ask God to give him an understanding mind. Thus, he says, he learned, not critically, but to a practical extent, the general teaching of God's word, and it was in this manner, and at this time, that his mind became settled on all those doctrines of which he afterward became so distinguished an advocate.

He became more serious in his deportment, and more diligent in his labour, lest the enemies of religion should reproach it on his account. He arose at four o'clock in the morning, worked diligently fourteen hours, and then esteemed it a privilege to walk three or four miles to hear a sermon. In this way he heard four sermons in a week, when the preachers were in that part of the country.

While he was thus diligently seeking instruction, Mr. Barber one day thus accosted him:

"Adam, do you think God has, for Christ's sake, forgiven you your sins?"

"No, sir; I have no evidence of this."

"Adam, do you pray?"

"Yes, sir."

"How often do you pray in private?"

"Every morning and evening," was the reply.

"Adam," the preacher rejoined, solemnly, "did you ever hear of any person finding peace with God, who only prayed in private twice a day?"

These were words fitly and timely spoken. They awakened Adam to the fact that he had not been earnest enough. His conviction began to be painfully deep. But he was yet to pass through a sore trial before he could say, "Though thou *wast* angry with me, thine anger is turned away, and thou comfortest me?" Through the cavilling of some acquaintance his mind became, for a time, shaken in its confidence in the divinity of Christ. He ceased to pray in his name. His distress became insupportable, and in his agony he cried out, using involuntarily the all-saving name he had forbidden to himself, "O God, hear, and have mercy upon me, *for the sake of Christ.*" The utterance of the name of Christ shot an encouraging ray of hope across his burdened mind. From that moment he began again to fix his eye of faith on the atonement, yet he had not the faith that secures pardon. His mind had not found the rest which flows from justification, but he was directed toward it; yet the nearer he approached the more fearfully the billows rolled over him. The malignant adversary of the soul makes his most vigorous efforts to destroy it when the penitent sinner is the most sincere and determined in "agonizing" to enter into eternal life. Adam began now to feel that sin was too heavy a burden to be borne. Like Peter sinking, when "the sea wrought and was tempestuous," he cried out, "Lord, save me, or I perish!"

Having gone into the field to work, he became too much distressed to continue his labour; he laid down his farming implements, and kneeling upon the ground, he continued supplicating the mercy of God. From this occasion he began to say, "Being justified by faith, I have peace with God, through our Lord Jesus Christ." So dear were the associations connected with this field, that, in the evening of life, after nearly fifty years of toil, of fighting, and triumphing, through grace, he attempted to purchase it, to erect thereon a cottage, in which to spend his few remaining days, that he might enter into the "rest which remaineth to the people of God," near the spot where he entered into God's spiritual kingdom. But the providence of God ordered otherwise.

CHAPTER IV.

THE IMMEDIATE FRUIT OF THE GREAT CHANGE.

Adam seeks the conversion of others—Missionary excursions—Labour for the children—Parents thereby affected—An old man's recollections—An humble chapel—Adam apprenticed to a linen merchant—Labour for Christ's sake—Rebukes sin—His integrity tried, and unshaken—An incident—Returns to his parents—His employer's residence—A brief review of the change, and its fruits.

YOUNG Clarke was now devoted to his religious as well as mental improvement. He read Baxter's "Saints' Rest," and the Life of David Brainerd, often called the apostle to the American Indians. The first gave him deeper convictions of the solemn truth of eternal things, and the latter stimulated his desire to do good to others. So grateful were the emotions of his heart for the undeserved love of the Son of God toward him, that he felt constrained to persuade others to enter into life. He commenced immediately, in an humble but efficient way, a work which he did not remit a day until God said, "It is enough," and removed his servant to heaven.

After the labours of the day on the farm, he went through the neighbourhood into the cottages of the poor, and, in a modest yet earnest manner, such as carried a conviction of sincerity, discoursed to them concerning the cross of Christ. When a whole day was at his command, he ascended a hill, and surveyed the neighbouring hamlets and villages, to arrange a plan of visitation. Then descending, he entered a dwelling, frequently saying, "Peace be to this house." He then inquired if they had any objections to uniting with a stranger in prayer to Almighty God. He seldom failed to obtain a cordial assent. He next invited them to call in the immediate neighbours. Soon these humble, neglected poor, with glad heart, filled the house. With a clear voice, he sang a hymn, spake a few words about the Saviour, offering to each salvation through his blood, and then kneeled and prayed. While his audience yet gazed at each other, wondering at his interest in them, and at the words he spake, he was off to another place. In this way he sometimes collected and addressed eight or nine companies in a single day, walking eight or ten miles into the country, and making himself a journey of twenty miles.

On one occasion he walked twenty-six miles with a friend of like spirit, expecting to enjoy a somewhat protracted preaching service. But other arrangements had intervened, and there was to be no preaching. Disappointed in the privileges he had anticipated, he commenced immediately doing good to others. Gathering the children about him, he addressed them. They were melted to tears. The adults having been reached by the word directed to the little ones, insisted upon an address to them in the evening. This he gave, and remained over the next day, at their earnest entreaty. Before he left, the preacher coming to the place, and seeing one so apparently youthful, and without the authority of the church, gathering around him the multitude to hear of the Saviour,—gently reproved him. When long years had intervened, and the boy had become a man, with hair white with the frost of time, he passed through this place: deeply affected, he called to mind the weeping of the children, the affection of the friends, and the chiding of the minister. "The people were pleased with me," said he; "for I was young, and little of my age."

These efforts will remind the reader of the characteristic labours of the Sunday-school missionaries and tract distributers of this day, especially those in our Western States and Territories, only that they have the advantage of a well-filled satchel of attractive books to distribute.

The preachers by whom Adam had been so much benefited soon extended the circuit of their preaching to the immediate neighbourhood of his residenee, and his father and mother—especially the latter—professed to receive much spiritual benefit from their ministrations. A chapel was erected about half a mile from Mr. Clarke's house. It was in the form and of the size of a one-floored cottage, thatched, and of unsquared stones. This chapel Adam assisted in erecting. He says, his father loaned the use of a horse and cart, and he carried stones to and from the cart, twice as heavy as was warranted from his strength, and adds, "If any one had offered me twenty thousand pounds for every twenty pounds of stone I carried, as an inducement to abandon the work, I would have rejected the proposal with contempt. Oh no! I would not have taken worlds for my interest in the work that was unfolding itself to my view in the salvation of my own soul and the good of my neighbours—so much of which was likely to be accomplished within that sacred enclosure."

The parents of Adam, not having the pecuniary means of educating him for the ministry, as they had purposed, apprenticed him to a relative, Francis Bennet, an extensive linen merchant in Coleraine. He had now been about two years a professed Christian, and was a member of the Wesleyan body. He was also authorized by the authorities of that people "to exhort,"—that is, to hold religious meetings, in which he might present to the people the practical truths of religion, without the form or the profession of preaching. Mr. Bennet seems to have been, in spirit, a man of the world, and it is not strange that young Clarke did not feel satisfied with his position. He, however, maintained his religious integrity. One of the servants, a profane, violent-tempered girl, greatly afflicted him by her wickedness. But after much effort and many prayers, he was made glad by her hopeful conversion. Another inmate of the family was an aged, decrepid woman, who had for many years been confined to her bed. She was much neglected by the servants, and was, moreover, perverse in her disposition, and was, in her personal habits, exceedingly repulsive. Yet did this young disciple visit her room every evening, for seven months, to speak to her about her soul, and to pray with her, rendering her at the same time such little service for her bodily comfort as his circumstances allowed.

He carried with him, at this time, a small pocket Testament. Being surrounded with profane persons, Sabbath-breakers, and triflers at serious things, he was accustomed to take out the Testament, and, with some well-selected passage from the mouth of God, rebuke the sinner—using the Word, as it truly is, as "the sword of the Spirit."

He sought other means of doing good. There were sermons in Coleraine, at five o'clock in the morning, when the itinerant preachers came to that place. Adam rose at four o'clock, and went through the streets to awaken the people, and summon them to worship.

After remaining a few months with Mr. Bennet on trial, Adam expressed to his parents a wish to leave the business, as it had become very irksome to him; but they were decided in refusing their consent. While the legal instruments of his apprenticeship were carelessly delayed, a providential circumstance interposed for his relief. Adam was employed one day in measuring and marking the cloth, and a piece came back to him, which he had measured several inches short of the required length. He measured it again; but still there was not enough cloth. Mr. Bennet coming in at the instant, said,

"Can you not make the measure, Adam? Let us take hold, we will soon stretch it out."

The conscientious apprentice hesitated.

"You won't do it, then!" exclaimed the employer, warmly. "Then you shall never measure another piece for me."

Adam stood by, and saw him stretch it, and yet fail to obtain the desired length. He then remarked, respectfully,

"Sir, you cannot charge me with indolence, dishonesty, or disobedience, from the time of my entering your service to the present period. I am ready to do any thing proper in itself; but this is not fair measure, and I cannot do any thing I know to be wrong." He then moved toward the door to take his departure.

"Where are you going?" said Mr. Bennet, relenting a little.

"Home to my father, sir," was the answer.

"You might as well stop the night over," answered Mr. Bennet, in a subdued tone. Adam went about other employment, but in a short time he was set at liberty from a situation with which he had no sympathy. The accompanying picture represents Mr. Bennet's establishment. It remained essentially unaltered at the time of Dr. Clarke's visit to the neighbourhood, a few years before his death, and was then sketched by a travelling companion.

We have thus exhibited the great change through which Adam Clarke passed, noting some of the circumstances which went before and followed it, in order to form a more intelligent opinion of the genuineness of that change.

This event is really the most important one in any person's life. Adam Clarke's conversion determined the important features of his future character, as it has passed into the records of the history of his life. He might, or might not, have been known as a great man, without this change; but such a man, with power to impress his generation for their good, he could not have been. We have seen that the ordinary means, faithfully employed, were blessed of God to secure the grace promised to all who sincerely seek it. The immediate work was marked by the presence of the Holy Ghost, producing a conviction of the reality of eternal things, and of the corruption and guilt of the heart, and leading to the Lamb of God, who alone can take away sin. We have observed the fruit which followed,—holiness of character,—love toward God, leading to obedience,—peace, which the world cannot appreciate,—a care to grow in grace and holiness. His ardent desire to save others, by inducing them to come to Christ, and his extreme conscientiousness, are worthy of special notice. When there was an humble service to be done for the neglected poor, either for their souls,—as when he visited from house to house; or for their bodies,—as when he waited upon the neglected sick at Mr. Bennet's,—he was bold to do it. But when an act was required of doubtful equity, then he started back, afraid to do wrong. These are legitimate fruits of the *great change.*

CHAPTER V.

PROVIDENTIAL GUIDANCE TO THE MINISTRY.

Early rising, studies, and labour—An incident of his first attempt to preach—Conflict of mind—Choice of a text—A severe trial of faith—Leaves home for Kingswood School, England—The sea-voyage—The press-gang—An incident of a stage ride—His disappointment on arriving at Kingswood—A story of a guinea—The first Hebrew grammar—Another trial of conscience—His first interview with Rev. John Wesley—His qualifications for the work of a minister of the gospel—His absorbing desire to do good—The providence of God observed in leading him to the ministry—Promptings of the Holy Spirit.

UPON his return to his father's house, young Clarke engaged in the labours of the farm rented by his father, and pursued eagerly his studies. He rose at four o'clock, and improved every hour. In addition to pursuing his Latin and Greek, he had, a little before this time, commenced the study of French. Even at this period, the desire to "intermeddle with all wisdom" was a prominent trait in his character. But it may be safely asserted that even his thirst for knowledge, which led him to despise ease and indulgence, was exceeded by his desire for the souls of the converted. We shall exhibit evidence of this.

One of Mr. Clarke's spiritual counsellors was Mr. Bredin, the preacher of the circuit, a man of sound judgment, and eminently pious. He was free from all extravagance of manner in handling the word of God, and to him his young friend acknowledged, in after days, much obligation for an early habit of presenting, in his public teaching, the plain meaning of the Scriptures, in opposition to a forced, allegorical interpretation. "This man loved me dearly," he observed once to a friend; "but he often treated me roughly, by putting me under a severe discipline." Mr. Bredin discerning, as he thought, unusual excellences of character in Mr. Clarke, resolved to put him forward in the public labour of the church. The following incident, taken down from one of Dr. Clarke's conversational narratives, will exhibit, in a lively manner, the method he adopted to do so.

"He asked my father and mother for the loan of me eight or ten days, and to allow me to spend the time with him at Derry. The distance from my father's house was thirty miles. Mr. Bredin was at Derry when I set off, so I walked the whole of the distance alone. Just before I left home, these words were impressed upon my mind: 'Ye have not chosen me, but I have chosen you, that ye should go, and bring forth much fruit, and that your fruit should remain; that whatsoever ye shall ask the Father in my name, he shall give it you.' These words I could not shake off; they recurred again and again—nor the thought that I might possibly be called to the work of the ministry, and that I might be able, perhaps, to preach some time, though hope was exceedingly distant. The day after my arrival at Derry, Mr. Bredin said to me, 'Adam, you must preach at "New Buildings" for me to-night.' I answered, 'I cannot preach, sir; but I will speak to the people.' 'You must take a text,' he replied, 'and preach from it.' I returned, 'I never did take a text, and cannot consent to it now.' After some words he peremptorily said, 'I insist upon your taking a text, and preaching from it, or you shall see my face no more.' The last sentence I knew not how to interpret. To pacify him, I went, literally in the fear of God, of man, and of the devil. I thought,—Well, I will go; I can only bring back the tidings, that I went, tried, and failed. I got to the place some time before the hour of preaching; and, not knowing any one, I wandered down the banks of a river, which connected itself with a beautiful sheet of water. My perplexity was exchanged for heaviness; I lay down on the grass—prayed—wept—and read my Bible. At first, there did not appear a text in the whole Bible for me;—I read, prayed again, and these words occurred: 'We know that we are of God, and the whole world lieth in wickedness.' My mind settled down on them as the text. It was not long before a man came up to me, and asked me, (as I had then risen from the grass,) whither I was going? I told him I was a stranger, and had been sent by Mr. Bredin, and inquired for the place of worship frequented by the Methodists. He asked, 'Are you the preacher?' I answered, 'Mr. Bredin has sent me, and I suppose I shall have to speak to the people.' The man measured me, apparently, with his eye, from head to foot, and then, in a tone of despondency, mingled with surprise, said, 'You are a *young one* to unravel the word!' I was struck with the man's manner, for he appeared serious, and with the word *unravel*, which seemed to have a good deal of meaning in it. He accompanied me to the place, and, for the first time, I ventured on a text, which was the one named."

"And how did you succeed in *unravelling* the word?" interposed a friend.

"Oh," said Dr. Clarke, "I spake to the good people about John being thrown into a cauldron of boiling oil, and coming out of it unblistered, with whose history I was pretty well acquainted. I noticed also the state of the world in its hostility to God and his servants, closing with some remarks on personal religion. The people pressed round me after service, one of them saying, 'You must preach at the Mount to-morrow morning, at five o'clock.' To this I assented, as all seemed pleased; and, accordingly, I spoke to the people the next morning, at the time appointed."

Though Mr. Clarke was, at this time, about

twenty-two years of age, and by no means to be considered incompetent, on account of his age, to "*unravel*" the word to an humble people, yet he had not now arrived at the period in which he was, in God's providence, to enter fully upon the duties of the ministry. There was in reserve for him a training in the severe school of experience. The course taken by Mr. Bredin, in urging him forward, might not have hurt such a young man as Adam Clarke, but will hardly answer as a precedent.

The next step taken by Mr. Bredin in his behalf was to write to the Rev. John Wesley, recommending him to invite Mr. Clarke to attend the school at Kingswood, in England, established by Mr. Wesley, and under his control. This brought a request from Mr. Wesley, now in the evening of his remarkable life, for young Clarke to proceed, without delay, to the school. Then followed one of the severest mental conflicts of his life. His parents were decidedly opposed to his removal thither. Though of age, he could not go without their blessing. His account of the circumstances is as follows:

"My mother was much grieved; her prayers were against me as well as her conversation. 'What is this,' said she, 'that has come over you? Your father is advancing in life—your brother is gone; we both have been looking forward to you to fill his place,—and now you are going to run up and down in the world like a vagabond.' *That* was her view of the subject. I said to her, 'Mother, I have made it a matter of prayer.' 'And so have I, too,' she replied, 'and the curse of God will follow you for it.' This was like a scald upon my conscience for some days. She spoke to me again upon the subject. I said, 'I do not wish to do any thing contrary to the will of God; and it appears to be in favour of my going.' 'What!' she replied, 'do you think it is the will of God that you should break the first commandment given with promise?' 'Honour thy father and thy mother.'

I continued to pray, to believe, and to fear; but had I known what I was soon to suffer I never should have left home. Having to go to Coleraine on business, where I stopped a few days, I found, on my return, my mother had relented. She, in the mean time, said to my father, 'I believe we must let this lad go; it may be, the hand of the Lord is in it.' Finding the way opened, I made some preparations for going. I had taken leave of some of my friends, and had privately packed up my clothes. Just before I left, I was walking and praying in the garden, when my mother came to me. I was afraid, for I knew not how it was determined. She submitted to my leaving home, and it was not long before I took my departure."

With a small trunk, a few books, and just money enough for his passage, and an economical living until he should reach Kingswood, he walked to the nearest sea-port, a distance of thirty miles, and purposed, when he should arrive in England, to walk from Liverpool to Kingswood, more than two hundred miles.

Nearly half a century from this time, when he was visiting near the place of his embarkation, he was engaged in a conversation with a Mr. Galt, on his early days, as follows:

Mr. G. "I recollect seeing you on the morning you left Coleraine for England."

A. C. "Are you correct in that?"

Mr. G. "Perfectly so."

A. C. "I was not aware of your being so old."

Mr. G. "I will convince you of it by a single circumstance. You went into such a shop," (naming the person to whom it belonged,) "and there bought a pair of stockings."

A. C. "You are right."

Mr. G. "I stood by you at the time, and when you left, I joined with the young men in saying, Adam Clarke was a fool to go to England to learn to be a Methodist preacher."

A. C. "I had no notion of being a travelling preacher; all I had in view was the completion of my education."

Mr. G. "Such was our opinion, and we affected to pity you."

We have introduced the above conversation to bring out the *purpose* which led Mr. Clarke to England. The ministry yet seemed to him, if he entered it, far in the future. But "The way of man is not in himself."

During this voyage to England, young Clarke was true to his own character and profession. He reproved the profaneness of the sailors, and to such an extent won the confidence of the captain, that, on his arrival in Liverpool, he constrained him to accept the hospitality of his own family.

When the vessel approached the port, a press-gang came on board. Europe was at this time (1782) embroiled in an almost universal war. The government of England allowed her officers to seize unprotected persons, and compel them to enter the navy, and perhaps to go immediately upon foreign service. Such an impressment Adam Clarke providentially escaped. There were on board two fellow-travellers, a hatter and a sailor. These two hid themselves, on the appearance of the press-gang; but Adam said, "Shall such a man as I flee? No, I will not distrust God?" and he sat down quietly, inwardly committing himself to God, in prayer. The officer of this kidnapping crew looked at his hands, asked him a few questions, and declared, with an oath, he would not do. The poor hatter was found, and carried away.

Mr. Clarke was persuaded by the kind family of the captain to change his purpose of walking to Kingswood. He took a cheap mode of conveyance. At Bristol, and during his journey from that place, he arrested the attention of those about him by his intelligence, modest deportment, and especially by his use of the weapon against sin, which he habitually carried with him—his pocket Testament.

His rustic appearance excited the mirth of one of the young passengers. He was soon drawn into an argument on important questions of morality and religion, and so impressed were his opponents with his ability and knowledge, that they earnestly solicited him to accompany them to London, on his way to Kingswood, offering to pay the expense of his journey if he would do so. But he declined the request.

On arriving at Kingswood Mr. Clarke was, in every respect, most sadly disappointed. He was told by the principal, that the school was not for such proficient scholars; that he had not received notice from Mr. Wesley to admit him; that the school was full, and, in short, he must not stay. Here, then, was an emergency! His friends were far away. He had come to England with sanguine expectations. He had about *three cents* in his purse, all his remaining cash. He could not be turned away; so the teacher gave him an uncomfortable room, and cool treatment, until Mr. Wesley should arrive, who was expected at Kingswood soon. The way in which God leads his servants is often, to them, overshadowed with dark clouds. So Adam found it. But the Divine purposes will shine through at last. Clarke soon found it so in his experience.

He was one day working in the garden for exercise. Another young man had just dug over the same ground. But in it Adam found a *guinea*. He carried it from one person to another to find an owner, and finally, not finding one, his tender conscience concluded it must rightfully belong to the establishment, as it was found on the premises; but the steward would not touch it, and, after the coin had been a matter of much talk and inquiry, it was turned back upon the finder's hands. With a part of it he bought a Hebrew grammar, and had a sum remaining sufficient for his expenses, until other resources were opened. "By means of that grammar," he says, "I was enabled to pursue a critical examination of the Old Testament, and while doing so made the Short Notes, which formed the ground-work of my Commentary."

The following is one among the many cases of conscience which occurred in Adam Clarke's experience. The stewardess of the school called upon him, at the table, to drink the health of some one named,—the custom of drinking healths being then almost universal. This he declined, giving as a reason, that the custom was useless in itself, and led to injurious consequences. It was replied, that it was one of the usages of her table, and that he need not be more scrupulous than all others. This reasoning did not answer for *him*, and he persisted. It was replied, warmly, that he should drink healths at the table, or drink nothing. The latter alternative he accepted, and to the end of his stay at the school, took no drink with his meals!

The arrival of Mr. Wesley at Bristol, a short distance from Kingswood, put an end to these vexations. Mr. Clarke walked to that place, and was introduced to this venerable man. He was received kindly, and, after a few words of conversation, asked, "If he wished to devote himself entirely to the work of God?" The answer was, "I wish to do and to be what God pleases." Mr. Wesley remarked, that a preacher was wanted for Bradford circuit, and that in a few days he would send for him to go thither. He then laid his hands upon the head of his young "helper," and continued a few moments in prayer to God, to bless and preserve him, and to give him success in his work.

On the morning of September 26th, 1782, Mr. Clarke left Kingswood for his appointed field of labour, after having remained there thirty-two tedious days. As we must now regard him as about to enter the ministry, we may take a glance at the steps by which he was led to it.

In his absorbing desire to do good, we see one of the leadings of the divine hand to the ministry. Not that every Christian young man, with whom this is a prevalent feeling, is thus directed; but it is to be so considered in its connection with God's providence and Spirit. Surely he, whose life is to be spent like his Master's, in doing good, need to begin and end that service, in a burning love for it.

Through the providence of God, we observe other steps to the ministry made apparent. At one time, the father of Adam Clarke indulged a hope that he might obtain sufficient education to be admitted as a member of the medical profession. This failing, as well as his hopes of having him enter the ministry of the church of his choice, his mother intimates a desire, entertained by both parents, that he should succeed his father as a school-teacher. But both had given up to what *they* conceived to be the directings of the divine will, in helping him to become a linen merchant. In this situation we have seen, that Adam did not betray his trust, but acted, though not pleased with his situation, as if it were the position of his choosing. The divine guidance was soon manifested, in a change in his employment more favourable to the great work upon which he was to enter, delivering him by an occurrence creditable to his reputation and piety.

Then came the opposition of his parents—their final acquiescence—the escape from the press-gang, and the friendships formed on board the vessel, and on the road, in confirmation of all this.

But most of all, perhaps, do we see the will of God indicated in the bitter disappointment of mind he experienced at Kingswood, where he had gone only to complete his studies,—the finding of the guinea, and the timely arrival of Mr. Wesley.

CHAPTER VI.

THE MINISTRY COMMENCED.

The labours of the Wesleys and Whitefield—A glance at the formation of the Wesleyan connection—The Bradford circuit—Frequent preaching—Studies on horseback—Induced to renounce the study of Latin and Greek—Mr. Wesley's advice—Feelings in reference to preaching—His apparent youth—The effect of a sermon at Roads—A reminiscence of that sermon—A curious history of his pocket Bible—His texts—Abandons, for life, the use of tea and coffee—Attends the conference at Bristol.

About the middle of the last century, the two brothers, John and Charles Wesley, and George Whitefield, began to preach the gospel with great zeal, gathering congregations wherever they could,—in the open air, in private rooms, and in barns,—as well as in the churches. A great revival of religion followed. In the course of the providence of God, John Wesley became the most prominent in this work. The people who, through his instrumentality, professed a desire to become Christians, he formed into "Societies." When the call for labourers became urgent, he employed men of piety from the mechanic's shop, from the farm, and all the common pursuits of life, as well as from the schools—to assist him.

These were for many years called "Mr. Wesley's preachers." As the "Societies" increased in number, he united several, often as many as forty of them, under the name of "a circuit," and appointed two or three preachers to preach in turn to each of them; the most experienced of these having a general charge of his colleagues, and being known as the "superintendent of the circuit." In the course of some years, the "circuits" multiplied, so that several of them were united and denominated a "district." Each society was divided into small classes, of about twelve persons. These classes met every week, to pray, and to relate their Christian experience. A person, called "class-leader," was appointed to instruct them in the duties of religion.

Another peculiarity of Mr. Wesley's regulations, was the change of the preachers from one circuit to another, generally every year. After his death these changes were made once in two or three years at least. Mr. Wesley had the entire government of all these societies, receiving or dismissing the preachers, appointing them to their fields of labour, and regulating all the affairs of the "Connexion." These preachers, however, met with him once a year, in what was called a "Conference," where all these interests were made subjects of free discussion.

Bradford circuit, which was assigned to Mr. Clarke, included three counties, and thirty-one preaching appointments in as many towns or villages, and was situated mostly between the Bristol and the English Channels, in the south of England. There were three preachers to travel this field with him, each making the circuit of the appointments every month, so that there was a sermon required of each every day. But the places for public service were generally far apart, thus requiring the preacher to be almost constantly (when not taking absolutely necessary rest, nor preaching,) on horseback, the usual mode of travelling at that time. Besides preaching, Mr. Clarke met the classes, visited the sick, and gave frequent public and private religious exhortations. During a little less than eleven months' labour on the circuit, he preached five hundred and six times, preaching one sermon every morning at five o'clock of the whole time.

As it is already known to the reader that he had, what might be called a *passion* for study, and perhaps known that he became eminent, in after life, as a learned man, the question may suggest itself, how was this passion gratified during these eleven months? That question he answers. He read on horseback, while going from place to place. In this way he began the study of Hebrew, committed to memory the grammar, and read the elementary exercises from the Hebrew Bible, and made himself somewhat familiar with Mosheim's Church History. To his Latin and Greek he began to give what attention he could in his moments of leisure, until the following unfortunate incident caused him to desist.

In a room, at one of the preaching places, where the several preachers lodged, some one had written, in Latin, a sentence relating to the vicissitudes of life. Clarke wrote under it a quotation from Virgil, corroborative of the sentiment. One of his colleagues, a pious, but unlearned man, when his turn came to lodge in the room, wrote under the quotation a severe reproof, of what he considered a vain display of learning. The tender conscience of Clarke, ever wakeful to wrong emotions in himself, and little suspecting them in others, especially in his seniors in the ministry, was exquisitely pained. Ready at once to assume that he had done wrong in the case specified, he fell upon his knees, and, praying God to pardon the offence, solemnly vowed never to meddle with Latin or Greek more! This vow he religiously kept for four years! At the end of this period he was led to see the rashness of his vow by a remark Mr. Wesley made to him, concerning the importance of making every possible useful acquisition, and of not forgetting any thing he had ever learned. He began to review the cause of his vow, and came to the conclusion that such an engagement was unjustifiable. Though the vow itself betrays a weakness, and want of proper consideration that is highly censurable, involving him, as it proved, in the violation of a most solemn promise, the reader may be inclined to accept as a palliation what, however, is no excuse, the sincerity and warmth of his misguided feeling in contracting the obligation.

Another of Mr. Clarke's colleagues was about his own age, with whom he conferred concerning his advancement in holiness. These young men, though not constituted alike in mind, nor intimate in other respects, sought each other's company, for the sole purpose of spiritual improvement. Clarke would often ride five miles out of his route, to talk with this sympathizing spirit on his daily experience in the divine life.

Young Clarke entered upon his public labours with much self-distrust. He says, he trembled in view of the audience he was to meet, and prayed constantly for the assistance of the Holy Spirit. He read the Bible upon his knees, and often with tears. Every where on the circuit, during these eleven months, was the work of God revived. He had commenced with great fear, lest his apparently extreme youth should hinder his usefulness. Appearing to many not more than seventeen years of age, he was frequently called the "boy," and the "little boy." But this circumstance was the means of advancing, instead of preventing his access to the people. Curiosity led many, when it was announced that "the boy" was to preach, to seek to hear him, who neglected the ministry of others. His ready utterance, fervent spirit, clear, forcible thoughts, and piety, which at once melted his own heart and the hearts of his audiences, pleased all, and secured a repetition of their attendance. The following incident will illustrate the above remarks:

At a place called Road, by a peculiarity in the arrangement of his work with his colleagues, he had not preached until the second quarter of the year. But few had attended the preaching of those who had preceded him. It was considered an unpromising field for the gospel seed. When it was rumoured, that a "boy" was to preach in the Methodist chapel, the young people came to hear in such numbers that they filled the house almost to the entire exclusion of the older members of the community. While he preached great solemnity pervaded the assembly. After the sermon the preacher read the hymn, beginning—

"Vain, delusive world, adieu!
With all thy creature good;
Only Jesus I pursue,
Who bought me with his blood."

He then sang it with a clear, melodious voice, with which he was then favoured. The congregation were deeply affected. That night, and the next morning, thirteen persons, young men and women, came to him, earnestly asking for instruction. The spirit of inquiry spread among the elder people, and a general revival prevailed from that time, through the vicinity. Some of the fruit of this sermon was seen after many days. *Fifty years* after, while Dr. Clarke was visiting a son at Frome, just before preaching, a man of gray hairs entered the room where he was sitting. He stood in astonishment, mingled with a respectful timidity before the venerable Dr. Clarke. "Can it be possible," he said, "that this is 'the tidy boy' who preached at Road, fifty years ago?" He then proceeded in a blunt, but honest way, to speak of his conviction under the sermon which we have noticed above; of his membership of the Methodist society from that time, and his present joy at meeting again, after so long an interval, the instrument of his salvation.

Mr. Clarke's constant companion at the commencement, as well as later in his ministry, was a pocket Bible. An item of the history of the one used on his first circuit is worthy of a passing notice, for the facts it reveals. After his death, it was rescued by a friend of Dr. Clarke's from an old rag-and-iron shop, for twelve cents. The margin was marked, indicating the chapters read in his devotional exercises, and the texts from which he preached. The latter were scattered through nearly all the books of the Old and New Testaments, indicating that they were selected as they struck his mind in the course of a consecutive reading. They are, uniformly, such portions of the word of God as would be readily understood by men of plain understanding, making complete sense of themselves, and apply, generally, to the daily experience of Scriptural holiness. We present them below, for such as may be interested to examine them.* On the title-page, in Mr. Clarke's hand-writing, was Luther's motto, in Latin,† which may be read—"To have prayed well, is to have studied well."

During this year he read Mr. Wesley's tract against the use of tea and coffee. He resolved not to taste either again until he could answer the arguments. As he kept his resolution of abstinence from their use until his death, we conclude he never found an answer with which he was satisfied, or had so overcome the habit as to be unwilling to resume it. The reader is perhaps aware that "taking tea" in England includes, as almost a matter of course, something like a social visit. Therefore he saved, he thinks, *several years* of precious time in declining invitations to tea, by the very conve-

---

* Gen. i. 27; xxviii. 15. Lev. xix. 17. Num. vi. 23–27; x. 29; xiv. 24; xxiii. 10; xxxv. 27, 28. Deut. iv. 9; xi. 13; xxx. 19. 1 Sam. 9, part of verse 27, "Stand thou," &c.; xii. 23, 24, 25. 2 Kings iv. 26; v. 12; xvii. 36. 1 Chron. 28. 9. Ezra ix. 8. Job xxiii. 10. Ps. i., whole; v. 11; ix. 9, 10; xxv. 1–5; xxxiv. 1–6–10; xxxvii. 39; lvi. 13. Isa. ix. 6; xxii. 20, to the end; li. 14; lii. 7, 8, 9, 10. Jer. xvii. 7, 8; xxxi. 9, 18–19. Ezra xi. 16–21; xiv. 14–20, Dan. vii. 13, 14. Micah ii. 10; Matt. iii. 10, 12; v. 3; v. 16, 25; vi. 9–13, &c., &c.

† "Bene orasse, est bene studuisse."

nient and satisfactory excuse, "I never take tea." Whatever the reader may think of this item of self-denial, he will mark the *time-saving* study evinced in the resolution.

In the summer of 1783 Mr. Clarke left his field of labour, and attended the Conference in Bristol.

He was at this conference admitted, in full, to the office of the ministry, without having served the usual length of time on trial.

CHAPTER VII.

TOILS, PRIVATIONS AND SUCCESS.

Removes to the Norwich circuit—Privations—Damp beds—Coarse fare—Small salary—An inhospitable reception—The benefit of keeping the Sabbath holy—An incident—The Sabbath breaker warned—Success, his support—An illustration, the pioneer of our "Great West"—Remarkable answer to prayer—Removes to the St. Anstell circuit—Two persecutors disarmed—Mr. Clarke's popularity as a preacher—The conversion of the celebrated Samuel Drew—His remarks concerning Clarke—Preaches to the quarrymen—Preaching refused at Trego—The manner of prosecuting his studies—Mr. Clarke and the shoemaker—Incessant labour—An opposer foiled—A timely loan of Kennicott's Hebrew Bible.

MR. CLARKE'S next field of labour was the Norwich circuit, including twenty-two preaching places. It lay in the east part of England, having its head quarters at Norwich City. There were three preachers beside himself to perform the labour, one of whom was Richard Whatcoat, subsequently one of the two superintendents or bishops appointed by Mr. Wesley for the Methodist Episcopal Church in the United States. Once a month, every appointment was visited by each minister, requiring two hundred and sixty miles travel. When they were going from one preaching place to another, which was nearly all the time, they were, with few exceptions, entertained kindly by the people; but when in the city, they boarded with the family who lived in "the preachers' house," and the steward paid (weekly) the expense, according to the number of meals which were eaten. As there was but one horse for the four preachers, they managed to divide his services between them; so that Mr. Clarke walked over much of his field of labour, carrying his saddle-bags, containing his few personal effects. But this was not the worst of the inconvenience under which he laboured. The people to whom he ministered being generally in the humblest walks of life, the entertainment he received, though the best his host had to offer, was often such as to expose his health and life. The winter was an unusually cold one, and the mere cabins—sometimes outbuildings—in which he slept, afforded him insufficient protection from the cold. The beds were sometimes damp or poorly supplied with coverings. So open were many of the places in which he lodged, that he carried with him coarse paper, with a hammer and chisel, to fill up, in a measure, the apertures. The people themselves were scantily supplied with poor fuel, so that he often retired to his sleeping-room cold; slept with a part of his wearing apparel on, and rose cold. The food was not only of the coarsest kind, but often scarcely sufficient in quantity to support nature; but in kind and quantity it was such as the donors had, and it was freely given. The allowance, by the regulations of Mr. Wesley's connection, was, at that time, twelve pounds sterling a year, or about $60, besides the mere article of food. From this the preacher purchased his clothes, and paid his incidental expenses. Out of this small sum each preacher, when in health, paid a yearly portion, as a common provision for sickness.

Among the outbreaking sins which he was called to oppose, none was more notorious than Sabbath-breaking. Even some of the members of the society greatly afflicted him by their loose notion and practice concerning their duty on this holy day. This sin he rebuked with his characteristic faithfulness, and his efforts were blessed, in several instances, with success. We present one example:

A miller, who ground on the Sabbath, attended the preaching. He at first became uneasy under the light he received concerning this sin. Soon he told his customers to call on Saturday, as he should not grind on the Sabbath. At this they laughed, and came as usual on the Lord's day; but they found him true to his purpose. They prophesied the ruin of his business, and assisted in fulfilling their prediction, by ceasing to patronize him. But soon one came back, then another, until most of his old customers returned, and many new ones; and he remarked to Mr. Clarke, "I am a thousand pounds richer than before I kept the Sabbath."

Another incident, which occurred, in part, under his observation, gives its warning to the Sabbath-breaker. A boy, son of the member with whom Mr. Clarke was then stopping, went out with two others, on Sabbath morning, with their guns. In endeavouring to get through a hedge, the boy of whom we have spoken having reached the opposite side, took hold with his mouth of the gun which the other held as he passed it through; it went off, and killed the latter, almost instantly. The son of the pious parent was so distressed that, in his distraction of mind, he endeavoured to drown himself. But he had been warned, for it was only the previous week that Mr. Clarke was writing the names of members of the society, to write them on tickets of admission to the love-feast, containing each a passage of Scripture. This boy, standing at the writing-desk, took up and read the one which contained the words, "Remember the Sabbath-day to keep it holy."

While toiling for the religious benefit of the people Mr. Clarke often laboured with his hands for them, in little acts of kindness, which, though unimportant in themselves, gave him access to their hearts. His sentiment was, "Be ashamed of nothing by which men's souls may be benefited."

But while we have endeavoured to give a faithful picture of Mr. Clarke's privations and toil in his Master's service for the poor and neglected, let not the reader understand that there were no circumstances to comfort and encourage him. Mr. Clarke found many, to whom he was the voice of God. While the word comforted them, they blessed the messenger. The lowly lot of those for whose souls but little interest had been taken, and to whom religion came as the only gleam of light in earth's pilgrimage, as well as their only hope of heaven,—was so elevated by such labours as he bestowed, that they became "rich indeed." To look upon this change, wrought by grace, inspired in his heart gratitude and love. So the pioneer in our Western country enters the forest, and there is no shelter for him or his children. The grounds are not cleared for planting, nor are the pathways opened for him to walk. But the brave pioneer toils on, nothing daunted. What has cheered him? Look now, on every side, upon that recent wilderness. There are comfortable habitations all around. Fields wave with the ripening grain. The village church, and the village school-house are near. These are, in part, his reward, and the hope of this made him happy in his privations.

Occasionally, Mr. Clarke formed acquaintance with those in the higher walks of life; and from these he obtained, besides much religious edification, the loan of books from their libraries, which to him was a very great favour.

Having laboured about one year in the Norwich circuit, Mr. Clarke received notice, August 7th, (1784,) of his appointment to St. Anstell circuit, included mostly in the county of Cornwall. To reach St. Anstell required a journey of four hundred miles. To defray his expenses about $5 was sent him! He started immediately on horseback. A penny loaf sufficed for his own daily sustenance, and his scantily supplied purse was made to provide for his horse. While spending a Sabbath in London, on his route, he, with many of his brethren then in the city, preached in the open air. A circumstance occurred during his sermon, illustrating both the providence of God, in protecting his servants, and the character of the times of which we are writing.

Some years after the present period of our biography, a zealous and useful preacher addressed Mr. Clarke in the following manner:

"Do you recollect preaching in Moorfields, London, during the Conference of 1784?"

"I do, distinctly," was the reply.

"Well, I was there, with my brother, and we had agreed to pull you down after you had commenced preaching, and ill-treat you. A former sermon of your's had reproved us, and we were provoked that a boy, such as you appeared to be, should teach *us*. As you commenced, I approached on one side, and my brother on the other. Strangely enough to us, each seemed reluctant to begin. I beckoned to him to commence the attack, and he gave the same sign to me. As the sermon proceeded, we were both disarmed of our resentment. I became deeply convicted, sought, and obtained pardon of sin through Christ, and am now striving to preach the gospel."

Such was some of the fruit of the seed sown on his journey to his new field of labour.

The St. Anstell circuit contained forty preaching places, each to be visited monthly. The labour was great, but the Holy Spirit was with the preachers and people—a general awakening commenced immediately—great crowds flocked to hear the word, so that the preachers were obliged, in many cases, to abandon the chapels, and preach in the open air. Several persons who subsequently became known to fame, were the subjects of this gracious work; among whom was *Samuel Drew*, who became a subject of renewing grace through the labours of Mr. Clarke, and an intimate friend until his death, which took place nearly at the same time with Dr. Clarke's. Drew was one of nature's prodigies. Though following the occupation of a shoemaker, his name became known throughout Europe as the author of works on the "Immateriality and Immortality of the Soul," "The Identity and Resurrection of the Human Body," and several others. His early conversion was doubtless productive of great good to the cause of religion.

Mr. Drew has left the following notice of

Mr. Clarke's public labours on the St. Anstell circuit:

"Multitudes," he remarks, "who scarcely ever visited the Methodist chapels on any other occasion, flocked to hear Mr. Clarke, and, at times, the places were so thronged that it was with difficulty he could urge his way through the concentrated mass. One instance of this fell under the writer's notice. It was at the town of St. Anstell. The room was so completely filled, that he was obliged to enter through the window, and literally creep on his hands and knees over the heads and shoulders of the people, to reach the pulpit. This tide of popularity continued to follow him without any abatement."

Although the regular appointments required one sermon every day and an additional one every third day, yet Mr. Clarke sought other places to win the neglected to Christ. Observing a slate quarry on his route, which employed a large number of men who were allowed *one hour* for dinner, he invited them to devote half of that time to listening to a sermon. This invitation they readily accepted, and, thenceforth, he ministered to them, monthly, while on the circuit, though it was so much taken from his already very limited time for studies which he passionately loved. He seems to have adopted the maxim of another great and good man, *i. e.* "Study is a good thing, but saving souls is better."

At a place called Trego, his well-intended effort to do the people good did not receive a kind response. He was directed by his senior preacher to a farm-house, as a point to gather a congregation. He arrived at the place toward evening, weary and hungry. The husband being absent, the lady of the house set before him a little coarse fare, and bid him welcome. But the head of the family soon came in, and, in a harsh manner, ordered him away. He would have none of his preaching, nor would he entertain him for the night, though the wayfaring man had no place of rest, without another exhausting ride, which would carry him to a late hour of the night. Yielding to the necessity of his situation, Mr. Clarke re-saddled his horse, mounted, and addressed the man in the following strain: "Sir, remember a minister of Christ came to your door with the message of salvation to you, to your family, and to your neighbours. But you refused his message, and thrust him from the hospitalities of your house. Now, as my Master bid his ministers do on a like occasion, I wipe off the dust of my feet, as a testimony against you." So saying, he took his feet, one after the another, from the stirrups, and deliberately wiped off the dust from them, and then slowly rode away.

Whatever may be thought of this proceeding on the part of Mr. Clarke, it is stated as a fact, that ruin came upon the man's affairs shortly; his family became corrupt and were scattered, and the man himself sank into the grave soon after, deprived of the farm from which he drove the messenger of peace. It is easy to suppose that such inhospitality and meanness were connected with other and equally offensive traits, which would naturally issue in the loss of credit and character, and in final disgrace and ruin, independently of any malediction.

The reader will wish to know how and to what extent, Mr. Clarke prosecuted his studies amidst these incessant public labours. He commenced at this time the study of geology and mineralogy, with text-book in hand on horseback, and a hammer in his saddle-bags. He dismounted at such localities as promised specimens of special interest, and, having broken a few, observed the geology of the location, and laid up the facts in his mind, he remounted, and in a few hours, (perhaps moments,) was delivering with freedom of utterance, clearness of thought, and divine assistance, the message of that God to man, whose wonders in nature had stimulated his faith and love.

Chemistry was studied in the same practical way. Moments of time were saved, while he was in the city, and spent in the laboratory of a friend, performing experiments, especially those concerning the process of refining silver, having in his mind, among other things, references to that process in the illustrations of Scripture. The reading necessary to such experiments was performed in the way, while going round his circuit.

Besides some ability in practical science thus early exhibited, there will be frequent occasion, in the course of this narrative, to show that Mr. Clarke possessed considerable mechanical ingenuity, combined with close observation of all the mechanical operations going on about him. The following incident will illustrate this remark:

Having, while on his circuit, called upon "one of the craft" to make him a pair of shoes, he gave particular orders concerning their shape, in order to secure a good fit, for, to so great a pedestrian, shoes, he thought, had greater need to be made to suit the *foot* than to please the eye. They were made, and, when called for, the following conversation took place:

Mr. Clarke—Looking at the shoes, "They will not fit."

Shoemaker. "How do you know that; you have not tried them on?"

Mr. C. "By my eye; it will not deceive me in this matter."

Shoemaker. "I defy any man to tell *by the eye* that a shoe will not fit, when it has been made, as these have, according to order and by the measure."

Mr. C. "I will try to put it on to convince

you of your error." The attempt to put it on was made without success. He then pointed out the difficulty, saying, "You should have taken a little out on the instep, on this side" (placing his finger on the part) "to have relieved the other." Honest Crispin saw it at once, and exclaimed, earnestly, "Ay, I have found you out—I have found you out—you are *a shoemaker*. None but a shoemaker would have observed this."

"But he might as well have called me a watchmaker," said Mr. Clarke, when, in a humorous mood, he was telling this incident to a friend, "because I took my watch to pieces, and cleaned it, as I did at one time; or a tinker, because I mended the bellows, which I found out of order at the preacher's house."

Very much of Mr. Clarke's learning, which he brought to an excellent account in illustrating Bible truth, was the knowledge (as we say familiarly sometimes) of men and things. He made his practical labour in science and mechanics, as well as his observation of such pursuits, a source of healthy recreation from more exhausting toil. But, notwithstanding such precaution, and the favourable influence of a naturally hopeful mind and a constant flow of cheerful spirits, his health declined. Indeed, preaching as he did, out of doors every day, in all weather, through the whole season of hot and cold, once or twice each day, and frequently *four* sermons on the Sabbath, must destroy any constitution not to take into the account his determined application to study, which filled up every moment that could be seized for that purpose, between four o'clock in the morning and ten at night. His removal at the end of a year from the St. Anstell circuit to the Plymouth Dock circuit, which now took place, was no doubt favourable, in some degree, to his health, in the *change* of labour which it secured, though it did not relax its intensity.

The same popularity, attracting immense crowds—the same divine blessing attending upon the word preached—the same providential care exercised over him, and the same application to study, characterized this part of Mr. Clarke's history—as were so remarkable in his previous field; and the reader will not be surprised that we add, the same weakness of body followed him. We will give a few illustrations of some of these items, and hasten on with our narrative.

Having an appointment to preach in Dock, at five o'clock in the morning, the year through, he went about with a lantern, in the dark winter mornings, to awaken those who he thought should attend the preaching.

He was preaching out of doors near a haystack. A man, whom the truth had provoked, came with his pockets full of eggs, to hurl at the preacher. His movements were observed by a friend, with a determination to interfere, if necessary. The persecutor took a side position, and soon, taking an egg from his pocket, lifted his hand, and squared himself for the attack. But a word arrested his attention, and he let his hand drop. Again it was lifted to throw the egg, and again he looked—listened—was arrested by the word, and dropped his arm. Thus he was foiled several times in his purpose. He then began to hear with deep attention. Seriousness sat upon his countenance, and he stole nearer and nearer, as he drank in the word. His eye soon became fixed and the tears flowed freely. Involuntarily, not knowing that he was watched, his hand stole into his pocket, and taking one egg after another, he dropped the whole on the ground. The man received lasting good.

A friend lent him "Chambers's Encyclopædia." This was to him a library of itself. It enabled him greatly to enlarge the range of his general knowledge, as well as to enter upon some new branches of study. But the loan, by a sister of the celebrated Dr. Kennicott, of a copy of her brother's edition of the Hebrew Bible, was the marked event of this period of his advancement as a scholar. It was now just published, and this loan enabled him to avail himself of its advantages several years earlier than he otherwise could have done. The careful study of this work gave him his first knowledge of Biblical criticism.

Thus far we have here exhibited the character of Mr. Clarke, in which the elements of a popular preacher, the traits of a hard student, the zeal of a devoted Christian, and the consecrated ambition of a mind of no common power, are plainly seen. A somewhat different sphere of action will enable us to view his character, in the next chapter, in a still clearer light.

CHAPTER VIII.

MISSIONARY LABOUR.

Sent to the Norman Isles—Commences preaching at St. Helier's, in Jersey—An escape from a mob—Another mob—Shameful conduct of a magistrate—The truth triumphs—His love for souls—Visit to the Island of Alderney—A primitive introduction—His cordial reception at Alderney—Conduct of the "Gentry"—Instability of popular favour—"A brand plucked from the burning"—Mr. Wesley's visit to the Norman Isles—Mr. Clarke's marriage to Miss Mary Cooke—Opposition from Miss Cooke's mother—Mr. Clarke's subsequent family—Cleanliness next to godliness; an incident—The reader introduced to Mr. Clarke's study—His Polyglot Bible—The extraordinary way in which it was obtained—Ill-health.

He who purposes to do the greatest possible amount of good to his fellow-men, will often find himself called, in the providence of God, to labour for that end in a way and in a field of which he had no thought. So it was with Adam Clarke, when it was proposed that he should carry the gospel to the people of the "Norman Isles."

The Norman Isles are a group lying near the French shore of the British Channel, the principal of which are Guernsey, Jersey, and Alderney. They belong to England, though settled by the French, who retain many of their own ancient laws.

Mr. Clarke commenced his labours in St. Hellier's, in Jersey, November, 1786. He hired, for a preaching room, a ware-house, a little out of town. Private rooms were also used for the same purpose, in more central positions, when they could be obtained. Most of the inhabitants of this place understanding English, he commenced preaching at once. For the benefit of such as understood only French, he wrote, and read a sermon occasionally, not daring to trust himself to preach extempore in that language, though he conversed in it readily. The word offered to these islanders was generally well received. But the common people, contrary to their usual practice, occasionally became opposers. At one time he went with some friends, belonging to the navy, to preach at a village, which could be reached by land, when the tide was high, only by a narrow beach. On this pass, a mob of the "baser sort" were assembled, to prevent him from passing. But the tide not being at its full, he crossed at another place, reached his appointment, and was nearly through his sermon before the mob was aware he had passed. They now came upon him with the fury of madmen. Many of his navy friends fled in great haste, leaving him to stem the assault as best he could. Going boldly out, he gained an eminence, and harangued them on the unreasonableness of injuring a man who came to do them good. The drums, horns, and shouting ceased; and, with the exception of a few missiles from the outskirts of the multitude, he was permitted to pass peaceably away.

He had a narrow escape for his life at another place. A mob assailed the place in which he was preaching, with almost every imaginary instrument of noise and of destruction. The congregation instantly hurried away, excepting the members of the society, consisting of thirteen persons. A pistol was twice pointed at the preacher from the window within a few feet of the pulpit, and twice the powder flashed in the pan. Not finding a ready entrance, the mob formed the desperate resolution of pulling the house down upon the heads of the little band. They had so far succeeded in sapping its foundation that it seemed about to fall, when Mr. Clarke said to his friends, "I will go out to them, trusting in God; they seek not you, but me." Finding him resolute in this purpose, a stout young man answered, "I will go with you." They opened the door, and were met by a shower of stones, but were uninjured. As if moved by one impulse, the crowd, who, a moment before were cursing, shouting, throwing stones at the house, and threatening to seize the preacher and cast him into the neighbouring mill-sluice, now opened a passage-way for him, and in perfect silence allowed him to reach a place of safety. The little band followed their pastor, "not a dog wagging his tongue." But no sooner was the prey escaped than the multitude, as if just aroused from a dream, broke forth into fresh violence, attacked the house, and left it in ruins. The next Sabbath, nothing daunted, he stood amid the ruins, to offer this persecuting people redemption through the blood of atonement. Again the mob assailed him with great violence. Gaining an influence over those nearest him, he succeeded in obtaining a hearing. He then reminded them that he was alone, unarmed, and a stranger; that they—a multitude of armed men—were thus showing their bravery! He had come to call them from wickedness to the service of the living God. He paused, and they began to shout, "he is a brave fellow,—he shall preach, and we will hear him." They did hear him, and many in that place found "peace in believing."

Though he had thus triumphed over the mob, he had one more battle to fight. It was with the magistrate. As Mr. Clarke was preaching out of doors the following Sabbath, near the ruins of his chapel, the magistrate came against him with a mob, and a drummer at its head. He seized him, dragged him from the pulpit, and delivered him to the drummer, who, with his companion, drove him from town, beating him at times with his drumsticks. From this misusage he was prostrate for several weeks. But he returned, to assert his right as an Englishman on English territory, to preach freely the gospel, and to see his enemies ashamed and silenced, and the word of God glorified.

While thus in "peril among his own countrymen," the love of souls constrained him to write as follows to a friend: "Never did I comprehend what is implied in watching over souls, as I do now. My feelings are so increased, and my concern so deepened to get eternal souls brought to, and kept with Jesus, that any backsliding among the people is a sword to my soul, and gives me some of the most poignant sensations. My conscience acquits me of a desire even to write a letter which is not necessary, or for the glory of God; for I find that in this, as in all other respects, it is full time to have done with all trifling." He says again: "I am determined to conquer or die. I have taken this motto from the Greek, and placed it before me on the mantelpiece: 'Stand thou as a beaten anvil to the stroke; for it is the property of a good warrior to be flayed alive, and yet to conquer.' "

In the spirit above indicated, he sought new fields of labour among the surrounding islands. That of Alderney was at this time reported to be without the efficient preaching of the gospel. There he purposed to offer the word of life. This intention having become public, it was rumoured that the governor of Alderney had threatened to prohibit his landing, and, in case he found him there, to transport him, a close prisoner, to a small island near, on which was a light-house only. In consequence of this report, the captains of vessels sailing for Alderney refused him a passage, and it was not until after much watching and waiting that he succeeded in obtaining one. No one had invited him to the island. Not one of its inhabitants were known to him. The words of our Lord to his disciples, when sent to the "lost sheep of the house of Israel," occurred to him: "Into whatsoever house ye enter, first say, Peace be to this house; and in the same house remain, eating and drinking such things as they give." Luke x. 5, 7. Thus impressed, he walked into the town, and when in the midst of it observed a poor cottage. Into this he entered, with a "peace be this house." To the occupants, an old gentleman and lady, he told the purpose for which he had came to the island. They bade him welcome, set before him a portion of their homely fare, pointed to a little chamber in which he might lodge, and offered their house for a preaching room. Being thus provided, he requested them to circulate an advertisement for preaching there that evening. The news of the stranger's arrival, and his strange purpose, spread with great rapidity. Long before the time appointed for preaching a multitude had run together. To them, though fatigued by his voyage, he spake the words of eternal life. Having dismissed them with a promise to preach again the next evening, he had hardly been in bed twenty minutes before his hostess awoke him, saying, that a company of the gentry had come to see him, and hear what he had to say, and he must come down and preach to them. He obeyed the summons immediately, and found the room quite full again. With great freedom he showed them, in his exhortation, the need they had of a Saviour, and invited them to turn from all their sins unto the living God. Great seriousness pervaded the company, and the Spirit of God was present to awaken. Before the next evening arrived he was again preaching to a large company. While at dinner the next day, the constable came in great haste, saying, that a number of gentlemen and ladies were waiting to hear him preach, and that one of the governor's large store-rooms, at a place called the Bray, had been cleared for that purpose. He hasted with the messenger, and found a large number of the gentry, who, however, had admitted enough of the "common people" to fill the place. To this attentive audience he preached from Prov. xii. 26; showing that the righteous was more excellent than his ungodly neighbour, however great, rich, wise, or important that ungodly person might appear in the sight of men.

The evening appointment was met; and on the following Sabbath he preached, by invitation, in the Episcopal church; and in the evening again in the governor's store-room. On Monday, greatly against the wishes of the people, who said, we need such a preacher and such preaching, he entered a vessel to return; but it was stopped by a sand-bar. So he returned, and preached that evening. The people rejoiced, saying, they hoped the vessel would remain fast in the sand until the next spring-tides! Many invitations, urging him to make their houses his home while he should remain on the island, came from the gentry; but he regarded the command, "Go not from house to house" as binding on him and persisted in accepting only the poor cottagers' hospitality, whose invitation was first given. On Tuesday the wind and tide favouring, he returned to Guernsey.

Thus was an effectual door opened for the work of reformation in Alderney, which resulted in the immediate spread of Scripture knowledge, and the establishment of flourishing societies.

Such labours and such devotion to the spiritual interests of men were not unblest of the Head of the Church. The following incident, among many which might be narrated, will illustrate this:

Mr. Clarke was preaching at one time at five o'clock in the morning, when a soldier wandered into the chapel. Though but partially recovered from the indulgence of the previous night, he was so powerfully wrought upon through the word of the Lord, that he went away deeply convicted, and, after three days of great agony of mind, was made joyful through faith in Christ. His wife, also, was brought to seek for the pardon of her sins, and both became worthy members of the society under Mr. Clarke's pastoral care. Not long after this event, when Mr. Clarke was recovering from a prostrating sickness, this poor, honest-hearted soldier called to see him. He sat down by his pastor's side, with great apparent tenderness and affection, and, seeing his pale face and emaciated form, burst into tears. The love of this sincere disciple of Christ, whose feet had been so wonderfully taken from the slippery places of sin, was a greater satisfaction to Mr. Clarke than all the flattering words of unconverted men. He felt that God spoke to him approvingly, through this poor man's happy change and holy life.

Mr. Clarke having been in this missionary field about eighteen months, was visited by the director of his labours, under Christ,—the Rev. John Wesley. Mr. Wesley, after examining the field and giving directions for its future improvement, returned to England, and Mr. Clarke with him. During this visit Mr. Clarke was married to Miss Mary Cooke, whose acquaintance he had formed when on the Bradford circuit. Miss Cooke belonged to a much esteemed and pious family, and was worthy of her distinguished husband. Her mother,—a widow, and member of the Episcopal church,—had valued highly the labours and character of Mr. Wesley, and had entertained him in her family, when he was visiting that part of his field of labour. Through him, his young helper had shared the same hospitality; she had learned to respect the piety and talents of the younger as well as the elder evangelist. But when his hand was offered to her daughter she was taken by surprise, and gave a positive refusal to the proposed union. Her only objection seemed to be, the sphere in which the suitor moved. To her, it was like turning her daughter upon the wide, unhonoured world.

All parties appealed for counsel to Mr. Wesley, whose high respect for parental authority led him to lean to the side of the mother. With his characteristic decision he told Mr. Clarke, that if he married without the consent of the mother, he could not remain in the connection. This was a strait place for the young couple, who were of one heart in the matter, and who both reverenced Mr. Wesley. They first laid the case in special prayer before God,—for (observed Mr. Clarke very properly) this was a holy cause, deeply concerning not only himself but the interests of religion. Mr. Clarke then made a particular explanation of the case to Mr. Wesley, which so far convinced him of the rightfulness of his position, that he lent his valuable influence in interceding with Mrs. Cooke. She was induced to retract her positive prohibition, but did not yield her approbation. Though for many years the mother refused a maternal recognition of Mr. and Mrs. Clarke, yet she lived, it is believed, to see, and in some measure to retrieve, her error in this protracted opposition.

Though out of the order of the narrative we may state here, that the family of Dr. Clarke was a numerous and happy one. He had twelve children—six sons and six daughters, half of whom (viz. three sons and three daughters) were living at the time of the Doctor's death.

Mr. Clarke having been married on the 17th of April, 1788, returned with Mrs. Clarke to his field of missionary labour. His excellent partner entered heartily into his labours, visiting the poor and the sick, and taking charge of the spiritual interest, in part, of the female portion of the society with which she was immediately connected. Having been educated in a somewhat elevated station in life, her sense of propriety was often offended by the habits of her female parishioners, whose temporal, as well as religious, interest she sought with great diligence. She laboured for their spiritual good in connection with the improvement of their social habits. Their want of cleanliness had been a source of constant annoyance to her husband, and led him, while sojourning with the kind cottagers during his visit to the island of Alderney, to find an excuse for cooking his own food, which he did constantly. "On one occasion," says a friend, "Mrs. Clarke took courage to speak to a good woman, whose children never appeared either to have had their faces washed, or their hair combed: 'Do you think,' said she, placing the subject in the least objectionable form, by proposing the question,—

"'Do you think your children are as orderly as they might be?'"

"'Indeed they are,'" was the quick reply.

"'Would it not be better to wash them?'"

"'Oh! away with your English pride.'"

"'Does not Mr. Wesley say—that cleanliness is next to godliness?'" answered Mrs. Clarke, hoping by this reference (as she knew the woman entertained great respect for him) to win her over to compliance with more decent habits.

"'I am thankful,'" she exclaimed in return, "'*that* is not written in *my* Bible.'"

Having recorded a sketch of Mr. Clarke's public labours in these islands, we will turn our attention to some more private matters, yet those of no less interest in studying the history of the man. We will, if the reader please, step into his study, and see if it often has an occupant, and if there is any thing accomplished there, amid such multiplied out-of-door labours, and among so poor a people, who afford their preacher and his family but poor accommodations in board and lodging.

We must be sure to enter the study by four o'clock in the morning, for if we enter later—say, at six o'clock, he may have been there two hours, and be already away at the call of other duties. We must also be there in those fragments of time—by others generally thrown away as useless—but which are like the gold-dust that the workman carefully collects, and in time makes into a solid bar—for these moments we must be on the watch, to know all the time Adam Clarke spent in his study. But at this time his preaching territory was not so extensive as in England. He was mostly in one large town, going occasionally from island to island, as we have noticed. The Hebrew Bible was found always at hand. The Greek Septuagint was now examined, and compared with the Hebrew, and short notes made in the margin of a Bible, for that purpose. He found in the public library of one of the islands a Bible, containing the text in nine languages, namely: Hebrew, Samaritan, Chaldee, Syriac, Latin, Greek, Arabic, Persian, and Ethiopic. He can already read the Hebrew, Latin, and Greek to some advantage. As the Samaritan, Chaldee, and Syriac are easily learned when the Hebrew is mastered, he has obtained the elementary books of these languages, and we find him now learning to read them. The Arabic, Persian, and Ethiopic were acquired at a later period.

Having sketched the history of Mr. Clarke's public labours and intense study in his present field, the reader is prepared to learn that he was, at times, utterly broken down in health. Indeed, it is wonderful that so prodigal an expenditure of strength left him any constitution for future service in the church.

So lingering was his disease, that the people were greatly alarmed, and proclaimed a day of fasting and prayer, and weeping "to snatch their poor preacher from the grave." The physician recommended a return to his old habits, on an extensive circuit, of much riding, and less application in the study. The necessity of this hastened his final removal to England, where we shall next follow his history.

CHAPTER IX.

CONSTANCY OF PURPOSE IN AFFLICTION.

A compliment from Mr. Wesley—The Bristol circuit—"In labours more abundant"—Mrs. Clarke—Mr. Clarke's opinion of frequent preaching—Visits the sick—An old pilgrim—A gift from an eccentric minister—Mr. Clarke's library—Removes to Dublin—Personal and family afflictions—Extreme Destitution—The "Stranger's Friend Society"—Becomes a student in Dublin Medical College—His knowledge of anatomy—Mr. Clarke at a book auction.

In July, 1789, Mr. Clarke was appointed to the Bristol circuit; and to the city of Bristol he immediately removed his wife and infant son. The reason given by Mr. Wesley for removing Mr. Clarke to that place was highly complimentary to the latter. He remarked to a company of Bristol friends at dinner, soon after conference, "I have a little self-interest in sending Adam Clarke and his wife among you this year; I desire their company myself." Mr. Clarke being made "Superintendent of the Circuit," that is, having a general oversight over the character and labours of his colleagues, and the business of the societies, his labour was even more arduous than formerly. His health continued exceedingly feeble, yet he abated none of his former application to the duties of the ministry. The following records may be taken in attestation of the truth of this remark: "I am almost wrought out with riding about, preaching, meeting classes, &c. Yesterday, I rode from Bath to Bristol, and back again this morning; met five classes, and preached once—have yet to preach twice, and meet six classes: to-morrow morning I return to Bristol, as we begin to meet classes at six in the morning, and continue, at short intervals, the whole day—and this continuing until the latter end of the week; but, blessed be God, I am willing to spend and be spent in such a work as this. I am almost prostrated for the present."

On another occasion he makes the following record: "At seven in the morning I met the Bride street society, and gave an exhortation; then preached at Guinea street; thence to Westbury, where I preached at two o'clock, and gave tickets; then back to Bristol—fatigued and wet—preached at five, and met the society; the next morning at five preached again, and then rode to Marsh, where, scarcely able to speak, I preached again, and gave tickets; from Marsh, the next morning, back to Pensford; from thence to Clutton, through a severe tempest—wet to the skin; Thursday to Kingswood—preached at five, and returned home to assist Mr. Hodgson to hold a watch-night at Bristol, but was scarcely able to move for more than an hour after I got home. I at length went to lend some aid, and Bro. Hodgson and I held on, till about eleven o'clock, when we made an apology for retiring, exhorting as many as conveniently could to remain, and sing and pray the new year in. Though preaching had begun at seven o'clock, scarcely a person attempted to go away. We left them, and one or two went to prayer. Just as I was passing to my bed-room, I thought I would go to the lobby window and take a last view of them, at which moment one of the singers was giving out a hymn. I thought the meeting would close for lack of persons to pray; I will go down. Mr. Hodgson advised me not to go. I hesitated a moment, but finding my soul drawn out in pity for the multitude, I said, 'I will go down in the name of the Lord.' Mr. Hodgson would not be left behind. I had before felt much of the presence of God, but now it was doubled. We continued singing and praying, and exhorting, until half-past twelve o'clock—during which time strong prayers and tears bore testimony to the present power of God. How excellent is the Lord in his working! How wondrous in his mercy! Lord, I am thine, save thou me! I am willing to breathe my last breath in thy work!"

Such were the *public* labours of Mr. Clarke at this time. Let us turn our attention, for a moment, to the domestic circle, and see how his excellent wife was engaged about this time, and we shall learn how far she sympathized with her husband in his zealous efforts to save souls. Upon this home-sympathy will depend much of his animation in the work. Mrs. Clarke thus jots down her own engagements: "I went Friday afternoon with Mr. Wesley to Kingswood, and did not return until Saturday afternoon. He is going again to-day, and my sister is preparing to accompany him. My dear boy claims my attention. I have a class to meet at half-past two o'clock, and to see tea prepared against the return of Mr. Wesley and his company at four. Then preaching at five; society meeting at six; also to see all things previously in order, and to sit as mistress at the supper-table at eight. So much for to-day. To-morrow I must see all in order for an early breakfast—to drive out with Mr. Wesley—tea again at five—attend preaching at half-past six, and then lead a class afterwards."

If Adam Clarke was enabled to accomplish an extraordinary amount of labour in the course of his life, he owed this ability, in a very important degree, to the judicious management and assistance of this excellent woman.

Lest the above records of Mr. Clarke's excessive preaching should provoke some young man to indiscreet exertions, we will present Mr. Clarke's opinion, in his old age, of frequent preaching, when the experience of life had instructed his zeal. He says: "He who preaches the gospel as he ought, must do it with his whole strength of body and soul, and he, who undertakes a labour of this kind thrice every Lord's day, will infallibly shorten his life by it."

In the above accounts of Mr. Clarke's *public* labours no reference is made to pastoral visits. These he did not neglect. He was especially attentive to the sick and aged. There was a lady in Bristol, who had attained to an extraordinary age. She was poor, and infirm, but deeply pious. With her he often prayed during his labours in that city; and some years after he had removed to another place, he called and inquired after her welfare. He was shown into the room where she lay, and, going up to the bed-side, he accosted her in the frank way in which he had been accustomed to address her. On hearing his name, she sprang up in the bed, and, grasping his hand, poured forth blessings upon him—blessings (he observed, in narrating the circumstance) which he believed he had never lost, and he had received hundreds through her prayers. The conversation proceeded.

Mr. Clarke. "At what age are you now, Mrs. Summerhill?"

Mrs. S. "I am in my one hundred and sixth year, and my daughter *there* is in her seventy-fifth."

Mr. C. "Though excluded through infirmity, from the ordinances of God's house, I trust you realize his sacred presence?"

Mrs. S. "As a substitute for the public means of grace, I *read* the Church Service daily. I can read the smallest print."

She then read a portion of Scripture without hesitancy.

Mr. Clarke formed many valuable acquaintances in Bristol, with men of distinction both in the Church, and in the more common employments of life. Some of his acquaintances, like himself, were just rising into notoriety. About this period he became known to Sir Humphrey Davy and Robert Southey.

Mr. Henry Moor, a man of prominence at that time, and subsequently one of the biographers of John Wesley, and an early friend of Mr. Clarke's, though much his senior, speaks of a visit to Mr. Clarke, while he was residing in Bristol. "He took me," says Mr. Moor, in his plain, clear, quiet way, "into his study, and showed me his library, with which I was greatly astonished, for my own would almost go into my saddle-bags. He had many choice books,—very choice,—among the rest a large Polyglot Bible. We conversed awhile, and I said, Brother Clarke, you have a nice collection of books, but what can you do with them? How do you command time to use them? On our circuits, where we have so much to do, I find it difficult to keep the doors open that have been opened; and sufficiently hard to retain any thing I know of the languages. How will you do?" Mr. Clarke smiled and said, "I will do as well as I can."

Mr. Moor was aware, and therefore told it in his conversations concerning his early friend, "That he obtained all his learning by redeeming the time."

In 1790 Mr. Clarke was removed to Dublin, and made general superintendent, under Mr. Wesley, of the religious interest of his societies, in that part of the kingdom. To be so far removed from his religious friends, and his associates in labours and success, was not agreeable to Mr. Clarke; but he received the appointment as a cross to be borne for Christ's sake. It proved a year of the severest trial of his ministry thus far, and, perhaps, we might add, of any subsequent period. The state of vital piety in the societies was lamentably low. Division of feeling and bitter controversies existed among the members in Dublin. The prosecution of his public duties was embarrassed also by severe personal and family afflictions. On arriving in the city, the building of the parsonage was in progress. He began to occupy it before the plaster was sufficiently dry, and he was seized consequently with a violent cold which resulted in a fever. Just previous to his own prostration, a lovely and only daughter was taken from him by death; and while he lay helpless and suffering, Mrs. Clarke was taken sick. He says to a friend, "My Mary and I were both ill of a fever at the same time, she in one room and I in another; and so soon as I was able to move at all, I crept upon my hands and knees to her bed-side, to see how she was, for I was too weak to walk."

Writing to a member of his family in England, while yet unable to rise from his bed, he uses the following language respecting the consolations of divine grace in this trying hour:

"You will doubtless wish to know in what stead my religion stood me in a time of sore trouble. I cannot wait to enumerate particulars, nor am I able. Suffice it to say, God did not leave my soul a moment. I was kept through the whole in such a state of perfect resignation, that not a single desire that God would either remove or lessen the pain took place in my mind, from the beginning until now. I could speak of nothing but mercy. Jesus was my all and in all. The Lord God omnipotent reigneth! Blessed, blessed forever be the name of the Lord! * *—For five months we have had sore afflictions, but the Lord does all things well."

A winter of unusual severity was no small item added to the inconvenience which his family suffered. His income, when his allowance was fully paid, was a meagre support indeed in such a time, but his people being generally of the poorer class, and being themselves pressed by the severity of the season, and rendered uninterested by their dissensions, he was left without even the full amount which he might claim from them. The recital of one touching incident will suffice to illustrate this sad part of our narrative. It is from his own lips, at a subsequent time. "We were allowed a little over two dollars a week for board. We were expected, it is true, to be out a great deal, but to this dependent state of things, neither my Mary nor myself could consent. Fuel was very dear and the weather was intensely cold. On one occasion, having neither food nor money, I went to my books, and selecting, with an aching heart, some which might be better spared than the rest, I repaired with them to a bookseller, who gave me twelve dollars for what cost me thirty-six; the hunger and the cold I would have borne rather than the loss of a portion of my small library, but that my wife and children should lack such scanty comfort as this sacrifice supplied, was a thought not to be endured for a moment."

These afflictions were felt, in their consequences, during the whole of his year's residence in Dublin. The reader must be curious, therefore, to know what he was able to accomplish in the work of saving souls, and in his studies, so diligently pursued heretofore. Scarcely had he recovered sufficient strength to be on his feet, before he might have been seen, "passing along the streets, a lank figure, with long hair, blue coat, and a cocked hat, appearing to see no man as he passed on his way, taking long strides, as if measuring the ground," hastening from chapel to chapel, to meet the hundreds of souls who waited to hear the word of life from his lips.

In pity to the many poor of the city who were uncared for, he was principally instrumental in forming a "Stranger's Friend Society." Two features of this society are worthy of notice. The only condition of assistance was *present want*. The members of the Methodist Society were not to be claimants, because other specific provisions were made for them in times of distress. Mr. Clarke had the satisfaction of knowing that this friendly effort for the "strangers" resulted in a permanently established society, being in a high state of prosperity, and patronized by some of the heads of the English government, at the time of his death.

To advance his education, he entered himself as a student in the Dublin Medical College. To the science of anatomy he gave special attention, as he had already done to geology and astronomy.

By his connection with the college, he formed the acquaintance of the learned professors, with one of whom, Dr. Percival, he continued on terms of intimacy until his death. Such ready admission of Mr. Clarke into familiar acquaintance, on terms of equality, by contemporary learned men (a familiarity which his self-respect and nice sense of honour forbade him to *seek*,) is an evidence of their estimate of his ability and moral worth. The reader will have occasion to observe that from this period of Mr. Clarke's history, honour seemed to *seek* him to the end of his life.

Mr. Clarke received, during his severe illness, a letter of condolence from Mr. Wesley, being one of the last letters he ever wrote, as that remarkable man passed away from earth a few weeks after its date. His high esteem for Mr. Clarke's talents and usefulness as a minister were often expressed in various ways, but most emphatically, by making him, by his will, one of the executors of his literary property. Over the event of his death, Mr. Clarke mourned, as a son for his father.

After this year of peculiarly severe affliction, in which the constancy of his purpose to *suffer* as well as to *do* God's will, was tried as by fire, Mr. Clarke removed from Dublin to Manchester, his next field of labour.

CHAPTER X.

CHANGES AND INCIDENTS.

The death of the Rev. John Wesley—The consequent change in the government of the societies—The "Deed of Declaration"—Ill health of Mr. Clarke and his family—Death of a little son—An encouraging incident—A hasty spirit reproved—A story—Total abstinence—His opinion of the sale of strong drink—Political excitements—Removes to Liverpool—An uncomfortable residence—The imprisoned leaf—Mr. Clarke attacked by two ruffians, and nearly killed—Great success in preaching—Mrs. Clarke's assistance in visiting the sick.

THE Conference at Manchester from which Mr. Clarke received his appointment, was the first after the death of Mr. Wesley. It was, therefore, an important era in the history of the societies which, under the Great Head of the Church, he had formed. We have, in another place, reminded the reader, that, during the life of this distinguished man, the whole "connection" was under his superintendence. After advising with those whose position enabled them to sit in council with him, he appointed the preachers their places of labour. By his direction, therefore, Mr. Clarke and his colleagues, had acted thus far. Now that he and his brother, Charles Wesley, were no longer in the church on earth, a new state of things must at once exist. The curious reader, not conversant with this part of the history of the branch of Christ's church of which we are speaking, may wish to know by what authority Mr. Clarke and his companions in labour, were now removed from place to place, and may need such information, fully to understand what may follow in this history.

Seven years before his death, Mr. Wesley drew up what is called a "Deed of Declaration," by which his people were to be governed after his decease. This "Deed" conferred the authority of Mr. Wesley on one hundred of his preachers, whose names were entered upon it, and whom he thereby appointed. This authority was to continue with that number always. When any vacancies occurred from any cause, those who remained were to fill them by elections from the other preachers. But this authority was subject to many qualifications and restrictions, as we shall see. This "hundred" is called the "legal hundred," and their name and authority exists, as Wesley formed them, without any essential alteration, unto this day. This hundred then received the power to say where each preacher should labour. They gave the nomination of the several ministers on the various circuits, to a committee of representatives of the people chosen by themselves, and in the confirmation of these appointments, they allowed all the preachers to vote with themselves. Thus it is now, and thus it was essentially when Mr.

Clarke was sent to Manchester circuit, where we shall now follow him.

We need hardly inform the reader, that he commenced his toil in this field in ill health. He soon suffered a painful bereavement. His youngest son, Adam, died in his father's arms after a sickness of a few hours. The grief occasioned by this bereavement never left Mr. Clarke. Whenever, even in old age, this little one's name was mentioned, or any incident brought him to mind, his eyes instantly filled with tears. His feelings would never allow him to name another child Adam.

Ever watchful of his own spirit, Mr. Clarke sought to correct a hasty spirit in any of the people of his charge. To one thus sometimes erring, he told the following story :—

Athenodorus had been many years in the court of Augustus, and being advanced in life, requested permission of the emperor to retire into the country, that he might pass the evening of his days in peace and privacy. On the wish being granted, he took leave of Augustus in the following words : "Cæsar, I have an advice to give thee. Whenever thou art angry. never say or do any thing until thou hast distinctly repeated to thyself the twenty-four letters of the alphabet." The emperor grasped his hand. "Athenedorus, thou must stay. I have still need of thee."

After telling this anecdote, Mr. Clarke addressed his friend in the following strain :—

"You will readily perceive that he who suppresses his anger until he has repeated twenty-four letters, is not likely to do or say any thing, which, from its precipitancy, would cause pain on calm reflection." The advice was favourably received, and profitably improved.

Mr. Clarke, from the commencement of his ministry, for the age and community in which he lived, took high ground against the use of intoxicating drinks. Fifty years ago, the time to which our biography now refers, the use of strong drinks, even by ministers, was very common. When Mr. Clarke was in Dublin, the general prevalence of drunkenness greatly grieved him. He set his face against it, and, to give his preaching the greater point, declined the social wine so universally proffered. For this he was ridiculed by some, blamed by others, as over-scrupulous, and hurting his cause by an ultra-position, and by a few commended as a consistent and sensible man. Soon after he went to Manchester, a young married couple came to him for advice respecting their worldly business. They purposed, they said, to open a public house. This, Mr. Clarke knew, involved the necessity, as then viewed by the public, of selling strong drinks. "I would die on a dunghill first," was his strong and indignant reply.

Amidst Mr. Clarke's labours and success on the Manchester circuit, he met with serious and discouraging obstacles. The dreadful civil convulsions which were breaking down all the ancient forms of society in France, were producing great excitements in England. Men had few calm thoughts about religion, amidst the heated discussions concerning the "divine right of kings," and "liberty, and the rights of the people." Many ministers became partisans in these contentions. Mr. Clarke, though decidedly in sympathy with the efforts of the people for a larger liberty, when sought by proper means, abstained from politics, in his public ministrations. He says:—"I kept the minds of the people occupied, in my preaching, with the doctrines of the cross. I dwelt everywhere upon the importance of a pure heart and its consequent holy conduct, and God blessed the word." His motto was that the minister was a man of one work, and that work was the salvation of the people through the blood of Christ.

After a ministry of two years on the Manchester circuit, Mr. Clarke removed to Liverpool in the summer of 1783. The law of the connection to which Mr. Clarke belonged, allowed the continuance of a minister in the same field of labour only three successive years. But at the time of which we are now writing, few were allowed to remain after two years. Hence Mr. Clarke's frequent removals. It will be observed that he returned a second or third time to the same field. The rule, however, was subsequently made to forbid the return of a preacher to the same circuit, until he had been absent eight years.

Though now again residing in a city, we must not suppose he lived elegantly. His residence he thus describes :—" The house is small. The street in which it stands, miserable. The neighbourhood, wretchedly poor and miserably wicked. So confined is our situation, that a poor shaving, which happened to be carried by a high wind into our yard, was kept prisoner there nearly six weeks, unable to effect its escape. I watched that shaving from day to day. Sometimes it would rise a little, and move from one spot to another, by favour of an eddy of the air. On one occasion, as by a strong and desperate effort, it rose about a yard, but, alas! dropped again. At length I set the poor captive at liberty." To the credit of his peoople, this uncomfortable position he was not required to occupy many months. While he was away, on the duties of his circuit, they removed his family to one of the most healthy, desirable parts of Liverpool. The grateful feelings that attended his surprise, when, on returning, he found his wife and family cheerfully and conveniently settled in their new home, were long cherished.

Soon after he commenced his labours in Liverpool, his life was nearly sacrificed to papal bigotry. He was returning from preaching one evening with his brother, Tracy Clarke, when suddenly he was felled to the ground by a stone striking him upon the head. He bled profusely, and was carried to his family, pale, fainting, and besmeared with blood. He lay between life and death for nearly a month. The wretched man who committed the crime, on being arrested, confessed that he was a Roman Catholic, and that he was moved to this act of violence, solely because he had chanced to step into the chapel and heard him preach the Protestant doctrine, though no allusion had been made to his own faith.

Having recovered from this prostration, he renewed his exertions, the Lord's blessing attending them. He says in a letter dated Sept. 13, 1793:—"Upon the commencement of my preaching here, the Lord began to work—crowds attended. Such times of refreshing from his presence I never saw. Should I die to-morrow, I shall praise God to all eternity, that I lived to the present time. The labour is severe. Nine or ten times a week, we have to preach, but God carries on his work, and this is enough. My soul lies at his feet. He has graciously renewed and enlarged my commission. All is happiness and prosperity. We have a most blessed work; numbers are added, and multitudes are built up on our most holy faith. Such a year as this I never knew. All ranks and conditions come to hear us. The presence of God is with us:—his glory dwells in our land, and the shout of a king is in our camp."

On one occasion three deists came to hear Mr. Clarke. He was dwelling upon the plan of salvation through Christ, his favourite topic.

He reasoned upon the stability of its foundation, the preciousness of its promises, and the exceeding love of Him who had purchased it by his blood, until his soul glowed with the inspiration of his theme. The deists listened, were first interested, then deeply affected, and finally became supplicants for that salvation they had, until this moment, derided. One of them, with his wife, an accomplished and influential woman, united with the society to which Mr. Clarke ministered. So the word of God was glorified.

While thus preaching, Mr. Clarke employed several hours each day in visiting the sick and distressed members of the society. In the evening he recounted to his wife the more especial claims some had upon female care; and, during the next day, she followed up his pastoral visits, as well as attended to her class. Their children were numerous and very young, and Mrs. Clarke devoted herself to their nursery, discipline, and their juvenile recreations. General visiting was thus prevented, though both were keenly alive to the enjoyments of the social circle.

Thus, with the co-operation of his excellent wife, did Mr. Clarke do all the work of a gospel minister,—preaching the word with all faithfulness, and visiting from house to house. How diligently he applied himself in his study during this period, will soon appear.

CHAPTER XI.

THE PULPIT AND THE FAMILY.

Removal to London—Commencement of the Commentary—Pastoral labour—Frequent and long walks—Mr. Clarke's preaching—A pulpit scene—A family picture—Another glance at Mr. Clarke at home—The conversion of Mr. and Mrs. Butterworth—A tract on "The Use and Abuse of Tobacco"—Removal to Bristol circuit, 1798—Publishes "Sturm's Reflections" and other works—Removes to Liverpool, 1801—Feelings at the age of forty—The conversion of a distinguished scholar—Painful sickness—Induced by too much labour—A visit to his sick room—Renews his labours with characteristic energy.

MR. CLARKE removed to London in 1795, and was continued in the field of labour (which included that city and the adjoining country) for three years. At this period he became settled in his purpose to write a commentary on the Old and New Testaments, and to make all his studies bear upon that enterprise. He commenced anew the critical study of the Bible, and translated every word of the New Testament from the original languages, examining closely the various readings, and comparing all with our common version. This task he accomplished, in addition to his other duties, in about one year.

He sought from every source every work

which illustrated the manners, customs, and geography of those countries in which the different books of the Bible were written. He was especially diligent in collecting volumes which were known of the literature of the East, printed in their original languages. He devoted his energies of mind to learn to read these correctly.

He never allowed his studies to prevent him from fulfilling any obligation in his more public character. To save time, he made it an undeviating habit to return home after evening preaching. The distance was sometimes ten miles, which he walked after nine o'clock, reaching home at midnight, and rising at his accustomed early hour in the morning. As he noted down the place where every sermon was preached, and the distance walked to deliver it, it is by this means estimated that he travelled, during the three years he was in London, over twenty-three hundred miles a year, for the purpose of preaching, besides his many and sometimes long walks for other purposes. He is spoken of by contemporaries, as making a marked appearance, as he started out on these excursions to deliver the message of salvation. His pale countenance, emaciated form—having not fully recovered his usual health—his hair worn long, and already nearly all grey—his long and quick strides—his eye intently looking forward, showed at once the hard student and the man earnestly pursuing a definite object. It is mentioned as one of his eccentricities, that he knew the number of steps required to walk from his residence to the chapels in the city. Perhaps this resulted from his habit of inquiring into whatever might be learned.

Having thus viewed Mr. Clarke on his way to the house of God, let us enter with him, and listen to one of his solemn appeals to the people. The place is Kingswood—the time Sabbath morning. The chapel is very large, and crowded. The preacher ascends the pulpit as if he felt at home there. His prayer is an earnest and somewhat familiar pleading with God for his gracious presence with the people, and his divine assistance in the ministration of the word. He takes for his text Psalm xxxvi. 7, 8, 9: "How excellent is thy loving kindness, O God," &c. Not a sound is heard, save that of the speaker's voice, as he describes how God gives those who turn unto him, "to drink of the river of his pleasures." At this point he raises his voice, and with deep emotion cries out—"Who is miserable? Who is athirst? Who is willing to be made happy? Who is willing to be saved?" A wretched man in the congregation, who had long hardened his heart by a course of uncommon wickedness, at this moment cries out aloud, "I am, Lord! I am! I am!" A scene of confusion ensues for some moments, while the man continues to cry in agony of soul, for God to have mercy upon him.

The speaker raises his voice again, amid the commotion, and says: "Listen." Instantly, all is quiet again. "Listen, for I have something more to tell you. Something for every soul,—a great, an eternal good. I am just going to open to you another stream of the river of his pleasures!" After a few more impassioned appeals, many are seen to weep, and there is heard the subdued cry of the convicted man amid the otherwise noiseless multitude. The service closed, the preacher hastens away to another waiting congregation.

After thus going with Mr. Clarke to witness his public ministrations, let us step into his family circle. We will seize the moment when he comes out of his study in the early part of the evening. His well-known voice, saying, "Come all about me!—Come all about me!" brings the whole group of his children, with a joyous shout and a rush, to obtain the first kiss, or the best seat upon his knee. Look now! There is one clinging around his neck; one hanging from each shoulder; one around his waist; one seated on each foot, and an infant in his arms! Seven in all, and not a child—with his merry shout and noisy glee—seems happier than the father, whose face fairly glows with delight. The play over, each kneels at the mother's knee, and repeats its evening prayers, and then the father carries them to bed, and, perhaps, playfully throws them in.

Suppose we take a glance at the home of Mr. Clarke under other circumstances. We find him seated in a chair, with one child on his knee, encircled in an arm,—another in the cradle, which he is rocking to repose with his foot,—a book in one hand, which he is attentively reading, and a potato in the other, of which, to save time, he is making a meal. Here is parental affection, economy of time, and moderation in diet, very beautifully exhibited in combination.

We have seen that, in Dublin and Manchester, Mr. Clarke's desire to make others happy, extended his exertions beyond his own family circle, in the formation of the Stranger's Friend Society. In London, in connection with several benevolent members of the Society of Friends, he formed an association for the distribution of soup to the suffering poor, in a time of great scarcity of food. At one time, so many were daily distressed by hunger, and so frequent were their calls at his door that he taught his children to lay by each a small part of his accustomed portion of food, and at night they were made to witness the happiness these little savings caused the hungry upon whom they were bestowed. Thus they were at once taught to feel for the distressed, and the way in which they could relieve them; the self-denial by which they purchased their satisfaction, making it doubly sweet.

We should expect that one so affectionate in

his own family would cherish the memory of his own parents with the most tender feeling. Such was the case.—About this period his father died. Ever after, while passing the cemetery in which he was buried, he removed his hat, observing at the same time, the most solemn silence, until he had passed the ground.

Let not the young despise this seemingly unnecessary act. The feeling which prompted it lay deep in the heart. My father! My mother! How much meaning in those words to a person whose heart and mind are properly cultivated!

While Mr. Clarke was labouring on the London circuit, with his usual zeal and faith, God gave him there also some seals to his ministry. The following is an instance.

A Mr. Butterworth, (son of the Rev. John Butterworth, author of "A Concordance to the Holy Scriptures,") had married Mrs. Clarke's younger sister. But to the time of Mr. Clarke's removal to London, Mrs. Clarke had not seen her sister since her own marriage,—so slight had been the intercourse between the families, in consequence of the mother's displeasure at the marriage of Mrs. Clarke. But Mr. Butterworth's good sense now interposed between the mother's authority and his wife, and he proposed a visit to Mr. Clarke's family with her. This was carried into effect. A mutual pleasure in the acquaintance succeeded, and Mr. Butterworth and his wife, who had never yet professed saving faith in Christ, went to hear Mr. Clarke preach one Sabbath morning at the "City Road Chapel." The following week they called on Mr. Clarke, and in the evening Mr. Butterworth walked with him to a preaching appointment, while his wife remained with Mrs. Clarke. When returning, Mr. Butterworth acknowledged that his mind had been awakened under the Sabbath morning sermon and inquired what he should do to be saved. Mr. Clarke engaged in conversation on this interesting topic, pointing him to the cross of Christ. When these visiters had returned home, Mr. Clarke began to relate to his wife the state of mind of Mr. Butterworth, and was agreeably surprised to learn that Mrs. Clarke had spent the evening in pointing her sister to the Lamb of God, she having been awakened under the same sermon. This intelligent and excellent couple soon found "peace in believing," became members of the society of which Mr. Clarke was pastor, and were distinguished through life for "letting their light shine," in their holy walk. Mr. Butterworth not only gave his heart professedly to God, but evinced the genuineness of that profession by devoting his fortune to the cause of Christ. He became a distinguished patron of the "British and Foreign Bible Society," and kindred holy enterprises.

After three years' labour in London, Mr. Clarke removed to Bristol circuit again, in

1798. About this period he began to be known as an author, by the publication of the works which we shall notice in passing. He had at various times sent to the press a sermon, or an article for the Wesleyan Magazine, but now his writings began to assume an important character. A pamphlet on the "Use and Abuse of Tobacco," attracted considerable attention, and ran through several editions. He remarked to a friend once, in connection with this work, that both his parents used tobacco, and he believed his father shortened his days by it. When his mother came to spend the evening of life with him, she continued to take snuff. He expostulated with her respecting this bad habit, but kindly and cautiously, lest he should wound her feelings without convincing her judgment. But his appeals in reference to health and religion, caused her to make the effort. After a short struggle she succeeded, and lived five years afterward, "preaching gloriously against it."

Mr. Clarke removed to the Bristol Circuit in 1798, and his first literary labour there was to translate and publish "Sturm's Reflections." He thus expresses his feelings on its completion: "I have finished the last proof of Sturm this day. I bless God, I am safely through it at last, after having spent much time and lost much, much health in the work. But it will live when I am dead; and do good when only the title-page shall remember me more."

A little later, he edited and published "A Bibliographical Dictionary," or an account of the most curious books in the ancient languages, published in eight volumes. Then followed "A Succinct Account of Polyglot Bibles," a small work, extracted from the preceding; and soon after "A Succinct Account of the Principal Editions of the Greek Testament."

In 1801, soon after these publications, Mr. Clarke removed to Liverpool. He was now about forty years of age. We are not surprised, in view of his unremitted labour, to hear him thus speak. "I was once a young man without and within: but the outward young man is gone, though the inward still continues. I have only to say, that if my natural force be abated, my eye grown dim, and my hair grey,—long—long before the ordinary time of life, Satan cannot boast that these preternatural failures have taken place in his service, or were ever, either directly or indirectly, occasioned by it."

Mr. Clarke often formed an acquaintance with men of distinguished learning and talents, who were not religious. In his interviews with them, he did not forget his obligations to them as a Christian minister, but endeavoured wisely and faithfully to win them to Christ. A curious circumstance gave him an introduction to Mr. Charles Fox, a distinguished oriental scholar; and a friendship was soon formed which produced important results. Mr. Clarke had received from a friend a curious stone brought from the East, containing an inscription in the Persic language. As he was not acquainted with Persic, he sought an introduction to Mr. Fox, carried the stone, and began by his assistance to study Persic. Mr. Fox was in heart an infidel. Mr. Clarke, in their familiar intercourse, sought frequent occasions to convince his judgment and win his heart, in favour of the Christian religion, but without effect. In this state of feeling Mr. Clarke removed to the metropolis and Mr. Fox to Bath.

Mr. Clarke wrote him an affectionate Christian epistle. Its spirit, and its frankness, accompanied by the Holy Spirit, touched his friend's heart. He yielded to conviction, sought and obtained the forgiveness of his sins, and continued, till death, (which occurred not long after,) a consistent Christian.

While in Liverpool the same active spirit for the promotion of learning animated him as in other places. Soon after his arrival in the city, he projected and formed a "Philological Society." But he nearly sacrificed his life to his intense exertions. He became subject to sudden attacks of illness.

Mrs. Clarke gives the following as the cause of one of these attacks. Such an amount of labour was doubtless well meant; but let none say that God requires such an expenditure of health, and exposure of life.

"All this has, I believe, been brought on by

too much labour. Last evening, to save Mr. Anderson from coming to Leeds street, through a deluging rain, Mr. Clarke preached for him, and met the bands. Saturday evening he preached at the Mount. On Sabbath, at half-past ten, he preached. Then met two classes for tickets, and came home to dinner; preached again at three o'clock; met two more classes, and met another, after Mr. Allen had preached in the evening. Monday he was visiting the sick nearly all the forenoon, and preached in the evening, at six o'clock, at Pitt street, to about fifteen hundred people. Tuesday evening he preached again, and met another class." Then followed the terrible night which had nearly ended his labours and his life together.

After a partial recovery, Mr. Clarke consulted several eminent physicians, who prescribed rest, especially from all mental labour, and pronounced his life in imminent danger.

We have introduced the above account of this sickness for two reasons. First, to warn the young, especially those beginning, or preparing for a professional life, against a reckless zeal either in the pursuit of knowledge or immediate usefulness. There is certainly a golden mean between a diligent improvement of time, and a disregard of the laws of our nature.

The second reason for its introduction, is to take the reader by the hand, and lead him to the sick chamber of Mr. Clarke. We have walked with him to the house of God,—we have heard him offer "the rivers of God's pleasures" to others,—will they sustain him in view of death? We have seen him happy in his study, seeking knowledge by which to illustrate the word of God. Will he be equally so, if God speaks to him from eternity? We have watched his joyful emotions, while gathering about him his much loved children, or folding his babes in his arms. Will his heart not faint if God intimates that he must leave them? We shall see.

Let us draw near to his bed of suffering. We may hear him say, "I feel myself on the brink of eternity. I know God cannot err; and my heart says, 'I have waited for thy salvation, O Lord!' and, 'All the days of my appointed time will I wait till my change come.' God is merciful, and I ask no other refuge. Jesus died, and is alive again; and because he liveth I shall live also." After a short pause, we hear him again say, in a subdued but pleasing tone, "I have from the beginning laboured in the work, and laboured to improve myself for the work. I have neither been an idler nor a busy-body; and now, standing on the verge of another world, what have I to boast of, or trust in? I exult in nothing but in the eternal, impartial, and indescribable kindness of the ever-blessed God; and I trust in nothing but in the infinite merits of the sacrifice of Christ, a ruined world's Saviour, and the Almighty's fellow.

Then what have I to dread? Nothing. What have I to expect? All possible good;—as much as Christ has purchased, that is, as much as heaven can dispose. 'The Lord is my Shepherd, therefore I shall not want.' My soul, looking through every crevice in her ruinous habitation, sees every thing to hope, and nothing to fear. Yes, 'The work of righteousness is peace, and the effect of righteousness, quietness, and assurance for ever.' Looking unto Jesus, I wait the will of the Lord, which will is, invariably, goodness."

Thus steadfast was the good hope of this servant of God, who, twenty years before, was invited by his light-hearted companions to go to Burnside for the "sport" of hearing a Methodist preacher. Perhaps the decisive course he then pursued, was the first step in the ways of wisdom.

Scarcely has he recovered from this sickness, when we find him visiting every day, except Sunday, a friend, ill of a nervous fever. He waited on him as a nurse, administered religious consolation, and, when he was partially recovered, presented him with a valuable folio edition of the Scriptures, saying, "There, I will load you with the word of God; it has cost me many a meal, but I would rather live with Christ's poor and despised ones, and be banded with them and their religion, than live in all the splendour of the rich."

Burnside.

p. 132.

CHAPTER XII.

UNSOUGHT HONOURS.

A vein of pleasantry—A delinquent class-member reproved—The man who was "Rich and a Bachelor"—The erring steward—A valuable cheese—Mr. Clarke outgeneralled—Literary labours—Honour from "The Philological Society"—The death of little Agnes, Mr. Clarke's daughter—His removal to London, 1805—His financial accounts kept by Mrs. Clarke—Multiplied engagements—Made President of the Conference—A committee of the British and Foreign Bible Society—Labours for the Bible Society—Corresponds with Robert Morrison—Literary honours from King's College, Aberdeen—Other literary distinctions—His feelings in reference to these honours—Additional publications—Engages in the "Record Commission"—The use to be made of honours from men.

THE following item is here introduced as a specimen of Mr. Clarke's Christian fidelity. It will be recollected by the reader, that we have said something about "The classes," so often alluded to. The minister having charge of a circuit examined the list of members of society quarterly, and those who had attended these weekly religious gatherings during the quarter, or were necessarily prevented, received a ticket, admitting them to the religious festival of the "Love-feast," as it was called, and being to them a certificate of continued membership. The custom is, (for it is *now* as it was in Mr. Clarke's day,) for the member receiving the ticket to pay the remainder, if any, of the sum he had previously agreed to pay towards the maintenance of the ministry. At one time Mr. Clarke, with a class-leader, was examining the leader's record of the attendance of his class, and receiving the payment. The leader laid down a piece of gold coin, to be put to a brother's credit. Mr. Clarke run his eye across the line against his name, and found "absent" marked uniformly against it. "Take the money back," said he to the leader. "The brother's *soul* is in danger. He never meets. Return him the money, and request him to call upon me." He looked upon the money as a bribe to preserve his name upon the class-paper. In this way, he would soon become an honorary member, purchasing that standing with money which others obtained by attendance upon those means of grace. Mr. Clarke's conscience would not allow him to receive such money, though for his own support, and from tho rich.

His reputation became thus established for unyielding integrity, and his decision was sought in cases of misunderstanding between members of the church, to such an extent, as to be a serious tax upon his time. But he seldom refused to listen to the complaints, and decide the question between the parties; and his decision generally closed the dispute. Once one came to him, complaining that a member of Mr. Clarke's congregation owed him a large amount for day-labour, and that the delinquent was *a miser* and a *bachelor*, but would not pay. "*A miser, and a bachelor*," replied Mr. Clarke, dryly; "two abominable things. But call at such a time on me, and you shall have your money." The man was curious to know how Mr. Clarke could give him that assurance; but he called at the stated time, and received all his due. Mr. Clarke obtained it simply by his moral influence over the miser.

If the readers are not weary of these incidents, and if they see in them, as we think they may, illustrations of character, they will be pleased with two more, before we proceed with the thread of our narrative.

A steward of one of Mr. Clarke's charges, in Manchester, was partner in a business firm. One of their creditors became involved in debt, beyond his means of paying. In this condition, the partner of the steward obtained from the creditor a bill of sale of all his property, thus leaving all the rest of his creditors wholly unpaid. This came to Mr. Clarke's ears. When the stewards met, the erring steward was in his place. Mr. Clarke, having consulted his brethren, said to him, "Brother, has your partner done so and so?" relating the above circumstance.

"Yes, sir," was the reply.

"Do you approve of it?"

"I see no reason to disapprove of it."

"Then, sir, your brethren see good reason why you should not be steward in the church of God."

The man instantly resigned, and retired, feeling, of course, sharply reproved; but he could not complain of the Christian fairness with which it was done. He thought of it over-night, and, in his reflections, the feelings of the Christian overcame those of the man of business. He came the next day to Mr. Clarke, confessed that his course had been wrong, and stated that if his partner did not relinquish the claim the bill gave them, and permit the other creditors to come in for equal shares, he would give up his part of the debt. His promise and recantation were received; he was restored to his office, and the cause of religion saved from reproach.

The other story is quite different, but equally showing the man. A large cheese was sent to Mr. Clarke as a present, with an intimation that the *centre* would prove the most interesting. The *cheese* proved to be good, but the *centre* valuable, for it contained a bank bill, of about four hundred and fifty dollars value. But for some reason, Mr. Clarke seemed to entertain the conviction that the reception of the money would compromise his ministerial independence; so he returned it to the donor in as delicate a manner as possible, saying that his family pronounced the cheese excellent, but he must beg to return the bill, as he was resolved not to accept pecuniary gifts. The donor received it, after a little hesitation, purchased with it a share in a trading vessel, in *Mrs. Clarke's* name, which for many years yielded her a considerable income.

But we must turn to more weighty matters. Scarcely had Mr. Clarke become settled, when he invited into his study several young men, who were striving, in indigent circumstances, to perfect themselves for the ministry. Between five and seven o'clock in the morning, he gave them such assistance in acquiring a knowledge of Hebrew, as enabled them to master its greatest difficulties. Thus did he permit no opportunity to do good to pass unimproved.

He published, while in Manchester, "The Manners and Customs of the Ancient Israelites."

By the request of its editor, he became a principal contributor to the "Eclectic Review," then just established. Several works of minor importance, from his pen, were given to the public at this time. The Philological Society of Manchester, of which he had been president, manifested their esteem for him in a manner best described by himself in the following letter to an absent son:—"You remember, my dear lad, my motto is, 'Be diligent, lose no time.' If I did not act thus, I never should be able to profit myself or others. During my late absence from home, the Philological Society held a meeting, not only without my consent, but without my knowledge; and what do you think is the result? Why, they have got two large silver cups made, each holding a pint, and beautifully ornamented with a border of oak leaves round the brim; and they have, in a very formal manner, presented them to me by two of the vice-presidents. They are each finely engraved with complimentary inscriptions."

While these tokens of respect were encouraging Mr. Clarke amidst his labours, he was called to pass through a very severe domestic affliction, in the death of his youngest daughter. The circumstances of her death are so touching, and they exhibit so clearly the advantages of religious instruction in childhood, that they will be interesting, we are sure, to all our youthful readers, and suggestive of profitable reflections to the minds of those more mature, —especially to Sunday-school teachers and parents. We extract the account partly from Mr. Clarke's biography, and partly from that of his wife, both written, we think, by the pen of the same affectionate daughter and sister:—"Being seized with the whooping cough, she had not strength of constitution sufficient to contend with the disorder; it fell upon her lungs, and bowed her down to the grave. During her sickness, her parents were chiefly her nurses. After writing for some time, her father would go into the room, carry her about until he was nearly exhausted, and then return to his labours. The child was remarkably attached to her parents, and though she often expressed her fears that carrying her so much would hurt her father, and nursing her so long would tire her mother, yet the relief both ministered to her in her weakness and pain, and the beaming of pleasure which displayed itself in the additional lustre of her eye on these occasions, were eloquent witnesses against the arguments her tongue framed into words.

"Lovely in her person, she was also peculiarly precocious in mind; she had acquired the art of reading without any trouble, and possessed a very retentive memory. Before she was four years of age, she had learned many portions of Holy Scripture, and could repeat numerous hymns. During her sickness, she delighted to say these to herself, as she was lying in the lap of her father or mother. The study, the pulpit, and the afflicted child, prostrated the remaining strength of Mr. Clarke, while the yearning love of the mother was manifested in every thing which could mitigate the suffering and exhaustion of their afflicted child. When increased weakness prevented her from kneeling as usual, at her mother's knee, to say her prayers, the distress of little Agnes was very great, and bursting into tears, she exclaimed:—'Mother, I cannot pray!' 'Yes, my dear child, you can,' replied her mother. 'How?' asked the sobbing child: 'I cannot kneel down!' 'Without kneeling, my dear Agnes, you can lie still and think your prayers, saying them to yourself; for you know God can see your heart, and hear what you have not strength to say aloud, as you used to do. You often lie there, do you not, and think of your father and mother, and talk to them?' 'Yes, I do.' 'Well, then, my dear Agnes, you can do the same in reference to God and your prayers; think of Him as near you, which He is, and then your heart can pray to Him as well as if you knelt down.'

"She was lifted into her little cot, which was beside her parents' bed, and, closing her eyes and clasping her hands, she remained in this attitude a few minutes; then opening her eyes again, she exclaimed with joyful emotion: 'Oh, yes, dear mother, I feel that I can pray,' and she ever afterward continued this silent posture of prayer. In the meekness of patience, calmness, and peace, this dear child yielded up her spirit on the very day she had completed her fifth year."

We are now entering upon one of the most important periods of Mr. Clarke's history. In 1805, he was once more appointed to labour in London. Here he found ample scope for the exercise of the ability, experience, and ardent piety of which he was possessed.

The London circuit, at this time, though not larger in territory than when he laboured in it before, included more chapels. From its centre, it extended twelve miles, each way, of course, being twenty-four in its whole breadth.

City Road Chapel.

p. 141.

Mr. Clarke being appointed the superintendent, resided near the "City Road Chapel," one of the most prominent chapels in the Wesleyan connection. The iron fence which ornaments its premises so neatly, was put up at Mr. Clarke's suggestion, and out of respect to his wishes. From this centre, Mr. Clarke walked to every part of the circuit, returning every night to his family, both to be with them, and to save the early morning for himself. Public duties now, more than ever, accumulated upon his hands, and would have confused and prostrated a less systematic and vigorous mind.

To relieve him of a part of his burden, Mrs. Clarke kept all the financial accounts of this extended circuit, with the most rigid exactness, methodizing every varied item in the simplest manner, while, by seeing visitors and every stranger, who would otherwise have necessarily taken up Mr. Clarke's time, she saved him from those frequent interruptions which are equally absorbing of valuable time, and unfriendly to habits of study. When from home, Mrs. Clarke also reported to her husband the contents of letters received during his absence, and acknowledged herself such as needed no special reply. Notwithstanding this valuable assistance rendered by his wife, and in spite of his early rising and scrupulous employment of every moment, he was almost entirely absent from his study. Mr. Clarke had now become so prominent a member of the religious body with which he was connected, and so much known to the religious and literary portion of the community generally, that he was finding the price, in a measure, of his fame, in the excessive labour he was expected to perform. At the conference of 1806, he was elected its president, the highest office in the gift of the Wesleyan connection, being an office conferring great honour and responsibility, and involving arduous services. Besides the duties of presiding officer at the conference session, its term of service extended through the succeeding year, and required the duty of a general superintendence of the whole Wesleyan body. By the president, the candidates for full connection in the travelling ministry were examined in doctrine, Christian experience, and call to the ministry, before the conference and the public congregation, and by him received a solemn pastoral charge before being invested with the full authority of ministers in that church.

The rules of the conference require, that a person, after having been president one year, (the term of the office,) shall not be re-elected under eight years. Mr. Clarke, in subsequent years, was elected a third time to this office,—an honour then without a precedent.

The British and Foreign Bible Society was, in form, organized at the "London Tavern," 2d of May, 1804, and about three months after its first anniversary, in 1805, we find Adam Clarke an efficient member of its committees. On his first connection with the society, he had charge of the foreign correspondence, but as the labours of that department increased, he was relieved by a learned German scholar, and confined his principal services to the oriental department. Mr. Clarke having remained in London as long as the ordinary rules of the Wesleyan Convention allowed, he was about to remove. On learning this, the Committee of the Bible Society addressed to the Conference a note, requesting that he might be permitted to remain in London and assist the Society. By a special act of the Conference the request was granted.

Few men are more generally and more favourably known to the religious world than Robert Morrison, the missionary to China of the London Missionary Society. Having been acquainted with Mr. Clarke before he left England, a correspondence was maintained between them for many years. After Mr. Clarke's connection with the Bible Society commenced, this intimacy was of great value in prosecuting his part of its duties.

While Mr. Clarke was thus labouring, in cooperation with the learned and distinguished,—a self-educated, untitled, itinerant minister,—he was surprised by the gift, by King's College, Aberdeen, of the degree of Master of Arts. This was conferred in the early part of the year 1807, and the next spring the same university followed it by the highest literary distinction in its gift, that of LL.D. Though these titles are not very weighty in themselves, at least, in our country, yet it was an unusual circumstance at this period, for a person in Mr. Clarke's sphere to be thus honoured. He was, at different times, made a member of the most distinguished literary and scientific societies of his own country, and of two in America. Though we must henceforth know him as *Doctor* Clarke, yet we shall find him the same simple, earnest Christian man, as before. At one time, in social intercourse he remarked, "With some of the most eminent of the literati I have an intimate acquaintance, and meet them frequently. My connection with reviewers, eminent booksellers, and the members of the Bristol and Foreign Bible Society, gives me an opportunity of gaining acquaintances, and hearing discussions of the most important and instructive kind. Learning I love—learned men I prize—with the company of the great and good I am often delighted; but infinitely above all these and all other possible enjoyments, I glory in Christ—in me living and reigning, and fitting me for heaven!"

In the latter part of the year 1807, while the full labours of a preacher, and an important part of the duties of a committee of the Bible Society, were still occupying the large portion of his time, he found opportunity to send to the press a work, entitled, "Concise Views of the Succession of Sacred Literature."

He purposed to add another volume, in the course of his literary pursuits; but this proved an exception,—a single exception,—so far as we recollect, to his enterprises of this kind. He did not finish it. But, as if Providence would in this even favour him, his eldest son, in after years, completed it.

But we have another record to make, of additional honour, and accompanied, as usual, with accumulated toil. In February, 1808, Dr. Clarke was recommended by the Speaker of the House of Commons as "a fit person to undertake the department of collecting and arranging those State papers, which might serve to complete and continue that collection of state papers, generally called Rymer's Fædera," begun nearly a hundred years before. The secretary of the commission, in addressing Dr. Clarke to engage his services, remarked that the work "required the habits of a Christian, a scholar, and a gentleman," and that "His Majesty's Commission had no doubt of his qualifications." With great caution, consulting his brethren in the ministry, and studying the indications of Divine Providence, he commenced this work, abating at the same time no pulpit nor Bible Society labour.

CHAPTER XIII.

THE COMPLETION OF THE COMMENTARY, AND CLOSE OF LABOUR FOR THE RECORD COMMISSION.

The Arabic Bible and Tartar New Testament published—A complimentary expression from the Bible Committee—Labours in the Record Commission—His opinion of Hume's history—A curious item of English history—Dr. Clarke's opinion of the Papal Church—A dignified official—Unenriched by his services for the Government.—*The Commentary*—All his studies made to bear upon that enterprise—its publication undertaken by Mr. Butterworth—The manner in which it was written—The deep solicitude which it cost—His feelings at its completion—A touching tribute of respect from his children—An incident, having a relation to the commentary—Objectors to the work answered kindly.

SOON after the connection of Dr. Clarke with the Bible Society Committee, the subject of a new edition of the Arabic Bible came before them, and was warmly advocated by him; and, finally, upon him devolved much of the labour of accomplishing the enterprise. Then came the project of a "Tartar New Testament." Of this Dr. Owen, in his History of the Society, says: "To obtain this Tartar New Testament became a subject of deep and lively interest; the preparation of types was diligently followed up by the Rev. Adam Clarke, to whose learned and judicious superintendence this concern has been implicitly confided. A scale of types, constructed by himself, and exe cuted with singular beauty, was submitted to the consideration of the committee, and a font was cast agreeable to the model recommended by Dr. Clarke, and sanctioned by the approbation of the president, (Lord Teignmouth, late governor of India,) and other competent judges of Oriental literature."*

We learn from another source, that so pleased were the committee with this scale of types, that it was ordered to be mounted and varnished, and preserved among the society's curiosities and treasures.

The laborious services of Dr. Clarke for the society,—requiring much time, as well as talents and toil, convinced its executive committee that he ought to have some pecuniary compensation. They, therefore, voted him about four hundred and fifty dollars, which was delicately tendered in a complimentary note. The money, however, was returned to the treasury, with a positive refusal of any remuneration. "To have done to the cause of God the smallest service," he said, "was a sufficient reward."

To discharge his duties belonging to the public records, he visited the British Museum, the universities, and the public, and many of the private libraries of England, Scotland, and

---

* Owen's Hist. of Brit. and For. Bible Society, Vol. I, p. 198, English ed

Ireland. Records were examined, and arranged, from the Norman invasion, A. D. 1066, to the accession of George III., 1760. Many of the assistants whom he employed proved incompetent, and some of those who were efficient left him through disgust at the vexations arising from the barbarous Latin, in which many of the manuscripts were written, and the mutilated and decayed state of others. But at this drudgery did Dr. Clarke toil ten long years, devoting to it, at some periods, successive days and weeks, and often his hours from five o'clock till ten in the morning. The result was four ponderous volumes, which were highly satisfactory to his distinguished employers.

The acquaintance thus formed with the sources of the history of the English nation, suggested the idea to him of writing a history of England, but his many engagements prevented it. He once remarked, that Hume, in the compilation of his history, was careless in the statement of facts. Mrs. Clarke was one evening reading to him from a volume of that author, when he observed concerning one of the alleged facts, "I have this day had occasion to examine the documents in which the truth in that case is contained; and it is as different from Hume's statements as if one should say sixty, and another sixty millions." He would often, in these evening conversations with his family, bring out many interesting and curious items, derived from these old, and nearly forgotten manuscripts. On noticing the "Caltonian Collection," in the British Museum, he observed, that he met with one record, in which William the Conqueror, and several others, signed with a cross(†), instead of their names. William's brother being the only one among the latter who signed his name, he was deemed learned, because he could write. Surely these old kings, who have filled so large a place in history, were less elevated in the true royalty of mind, than the children of our Sunday-schools!

It may naturally be supposed that duties so laborious as were involved in the commission, and requiring so great learning and talents, would, under the English government, enrich the commissioned; but he says, "I give up my salary with my work; I looked for nothing, and came out of the office unenriched; for I would in no case hold a *sinecure*." On resigning, in consequence of ill health and other hindrances, he was asked, by the commissioners, delicately but very meaningly, if they could do any thing for him—if he had a son to whom they could be of service. "Yes," replied the Doctor, "if you have work for him to do; but no son of mine shall, with my consent, recieve a salary for which he does not labour." His eldest son was immediately put into the record office.

During all these ten years of toil in the

government service, the Commentary, the great work of his life, was on his hands. Of this we will now give a summary account, anticipating, in a part of it, for the sake of unity of subject, the time of our narrative.

Amidst Dr. Clarke's numerous other engagements, in sickness and health, from the dawnings of his manhood, until he saw the last page in the hands of the printer, he ever kept in mind this enterprise. Into other literary engagements he entered, because they were connected with this. We shall see from his own account, that both health and spirits often failed for a time, but nothing but the entire and continued loss of health, or of life itself, could shake his purpose. Every study and labour of his life, except perhaps the "Record Committee," was made subservient to it. Having now arrived at a period when the manuscripts were about ready for the press, the expense of giving it to the world was beyond his means, and he seems, for some reason, to have hesitated to present the responsibility to any publishing house. At this juncture, his brother-in-law, Joseph Butterworth, offered to assume the whole responsibility. He issued circulars, and made the contracts, investing in the enterprise a large portion of his fortune. The first part of the work appeared in September, 1810. An edition of eleven thousand copies was immediately struck off, which did not supply the market. At different periods, for fifteen years, successive portions were sent to the press. His feel ings, at the conclusion of this great undertaking, are best given in his own words, taken from his remarks at the close of Malachi, the part of the commentary last written. "In this arduous labour I have had no assistant, not even a single week's help from an *amanuensis*, no person to look for me common places, or to refer to an ancient author, to find out the place, or to transcribe a passage of Latin, or Greek, or any other language which my memory had generally recalled, or to verify a quotation; the help excepted, which I received in the chronological department from my own nephew, Mr. John Edward Clarke; I have laboured alone for nearly twenty-five years previously to the work being sent to the press, and fifteen years have been employed in bringing it through the press to the public; and thus about forty years of my life have been consumed; and from this the reader will at once perceive that the work, whether well or ill executed, has not been done in a careless or precipitate manner, nor have any means within my reach been neglected, to make it, in every respect, as far as possible, what the title page promises, "*A Help to the better understanding of the Sacred Writings.*" Thus, through the merciful help of God, my labour in this field terminates,—a labour, which, if it were yet to commence, with the knowledge I now have of its difficulty, and, in many respects, my inadequate means, millions even of the gold of Ophir, and all the honours that can come from man, could not induce me to undertake. Now it is finished, I regret not the labour."

The members of his family bore witness to his solicitude and labour, before his task was done. Often, when perplexed with a passage of Scripture which he wished to interpret, had they knocked at his study door, and their knock been unheeded because not noticed, so absorbed was he in his mental exercise—entering, they have found him on his knees, his pen and paper lying before him, wrestling with the "Father of Lights," to send the illuminating Spirit into his mind. On his knees was the last sentence of the commentary written,—and in that humble posture he continued, until he had, with a heart overflowing with deep emotion, rendered thanks to his Heavenly Father, that his life and health had been spared, and his sensible presence given, to bring the work to a close.

Having thus first rendered thanks to God, he hastened to call his family to participate in his joy. Taking his youngest son into the study he said to him, "This, Joseph, is the happiest period I have enjoyed for years; I have put the last hand to my commentary; I have written the last word of the work; I have put away the chains which would remind me of my bondage; and there, I have returned the deep thanks of a grateful soul to God who has shown me so great and continued kindness;

I shall now go into the parlour, tell my good news to the rest, and enjoy myself for the day."

The gratitude and sympathy of his children at this auspicious event, was shown in a very touching manner. The parents were invited to the residence of the two oldest sons. The whole family were gathered around a well-spread table. The dinner being over, an elegant silver vase was brought, covered, and set at the head of the table. His eldest son then arose, and in the name of each and all the family, presented it to the honoured father. He was taken entirely by surprise, and for some moments his emotions were too intense for utterance. Rising slowly, and placing his hands upon this token of his children's love, he pronounced upon each of them, individually, his blessing. He then addressed them as a company, in strains of affectionate tenderness, in the name of their much loved mother and himself.

The following incidents, having a relation to the account of the Commentary, illustrate some characteristics of Dr. Clarke. A friend, knowing his reluctance to receive money as a gift, put into his hands twenty-five dollars, intimating that, as he could not himself honour God by writing an illustration of his Holy Word, he wished to have a part in such a work, though written by another, and therefore begged him to purchase with the money pens and paper for the manuscript of his commentary. The money was received. Many years afterward, when the work was coming from the press, the doctor sent his friend the comment on Matthew, reminding him of the circumstance, and adding: "The money has been applied precisely as you wished."

As might be expected, the work occasioned numerous expressions of opinions with regard to its merit; by some it was commended, by others condemned, not always in the kindest, nor most liberal spirit. These he seldom noticed. He was opposed, from his mental taste and religious principles, to controversy. On one occasion he remarked to a friend:—"Mr. H—— has been attacking me, finding an abundance of faults with my Commentary, not one of which he has proved; but my maxim is, you know, always to answer such persons kindly, having reason to believe that by this method some have not only been softened, but made ashamed of themselves. I find it not only impossible to please everybody, but that it is scarcely possible to please anybody. Woe to him who writes a Commentary, and consults his own judgment and conscience in the work! All hail thou truth of Jehovah! Be thou established forever!'

CHAPTER XIV.

LABOURS MORE ABUNDANT.

Elected librarian of the Surrey Institute—Publishes "Harmer's Observations"—Other Publications—A great enterprise projected—Anecdotes of Dr. Clarke's love for the Bible—Second time president of the conference—Anecdotes of Dr. Clarke and the tobacco users—Labours for the Wesleyan Missionary Society—Occasional Sermons—A reproof—Reminiscences—Dr. Clarke at fifty-five years of age.

WHILE in London, Dr. Clarke was induced to stand as a candidate for the office of librarian in the Surrey Institute, which was a public literary institute of some note. The office was, at the time, the subject of bitter, sectarian controversy, and the popularity of his name was used, to subdue party violence. He was elected, and occupied the position less than a year, and resigned it in disgust. He says of its duties:—"I have all the books in both libraries to provide; I have to travel from shop to shop to examine books,—to compare the different prices of the same article, before I purchase; I have lectures, and the plan of lectures, and even their matter to arrange; I have to construct the whole machine, and give it its proper momentum and direction;—to be incessant in labour, and to employ all my bibliographical and philosophical knowledge in those things; and, as I have taken them in hand, I shall do them, if God spare my life."

On leaving the office, he refused to receive a penny of the salary which belonged to it. We infer that the reason was, that party censure should not have even an unreasonable occasion to say that he had held the place for personal profit. His successor in the institution was the distinguished Rev. T. H. Horne, author of "An Introduction to the Critical Study of the Holy Scriptures."

While the Record Commission and Commentary were yet occupying his mind, Dr. Clarke prepared for the press an edition of "Harmer's Observations on various passages of Scripture," adding tables of contents and observations of his own.

As if his literary engagements were not enough, there were placed in his hands the papers and letters of Archbishop Sharp, and of Granville Sharp, embracing many important matters relating to the state, to religion, and to literature—for him to arrange, select, condemn, or approve. This task was also undertaken and executed.

Another labour performed was a draft of a library for the Bible Society, to be sent to India for the use of the translators of the Scriptures in that country.

Not far from the same period, an edition of Butterworth's Concordance, enlarged and improved, by his labours came from the press.

Besides what he did publish, Dr. Clarke, with a learned friend, proposed to contribute their influence and assistance in securing the publication of the London Polyglot, a very expensive and scarce work. To secure this object, he published a tract upon the subject as early as 1810, and sent it to the learned men in Great Britain and on the continent. So zealous had he become in this undertaking, that it was not abandoned until many years afterwards. The work was one of immense cost of both money and time. The expense of the proposed edition was estimated at four hundred and forty-four thousand dollars, and it was calculated that seven years would be required to carry it through the press.

Thus the *Bible*, directly or indirectly, was connected with all his efforts. We are not surprised, therefore, to learn that at all times and in all places, he showed a most profound reverence for this Holy Book. When he read it in his family devotions, it was always standing—"the more," as he said, "to reverence it."

While preaching once in his usual style, he paused for a few moments, and, without the least air of ostentation, said—his eyes beaming meanwhile with benignant pleasure on an attentive auditory—"Some of you may have seen Adam Clarke before,—more of you have heard of him, and among other things, you may have been told that he has studied hard, and read much; but he has to tell you, that he never met with but ONE book in his life that he could hug to his heart, and it is this blessed Book of God (taking up the Bible at the time that had lain open before him, and placing it to his breast, with the endearing embrace of a mother clasping her child to her bosom.) The effect was electrical. A simultaneous burst of half-stifled applause was heard through the whole congregation—men, women and children weeping, while his own eyes were brimmed with tears."

As he sat with a friend in his study at one time, the servant girl, in passing out, set the door open by placing against it a large Bible. Rising calmly, Dr. Clarke supplied its place with something more appropriate, saying, as he placed the Holy Book on the shelf: "Poor Betty is ignorant, and has no religion, or she would not treat God's Word so."

At the conference of 1814, Dr. Clarke was again chosen president. This office imposed upon him great additional duties. Among these duties, as we have stated, was the task of examining, before the conference and the public congregation, the candidates for full membership. Besides other matters, it is required, by the rules of the Wesleyan body, that these candidates shall not indulge in the use of tobacco in any form. One of the young men now claiming admission, the doctor knew to be an immoderate smoker, and whom, as he highly respected him, he determined to rescue, if possible, from the pernicious habit. The young men being arranged before the president, he addressed them, in turn, on the subject, and coming to the young man in question, the following conversation took place:—

"Do you use tobacco in any form, brother?"

"A little, sir."

"You must give it up."

"I use it for the sake of my health, sir."

"Our rule is against it, and I cannot admit you unless you will give it up."

"Well, sir, I will try to give it up."

"An attempt will do nothing, unless persevered in."

"I think it hard, sir, where health requires it."

"Our rule knows no exception, and I would not, in the situation in which I am placed, admit my own father—no not an angel from heaven, without a pledge of total abandonment. You can take time to consider it; do nothing rashly; if, after you have thought upon it a day or two, or another year, you think you can conscientiously give the pledge, you can then be received."

The candidate began to feel that the affair was assuming a serious aspect. He must either be put back on trial, or abandon his place in the conference, or give the required pledge. After a little pause he answered, "Well, sir, I feel inclined to relinquish it."

"Do you solemnly promise it?"

"I do, sir."

"Express yourself clearly, brother. Am I to understand you to bind yourself to give it up *now*, only for a short period, and be at liberty to resume it? There is no mental reservation, is there?"

"I cannot say, sir, what circumstances of health, &c., might occur to call for it; but I intend it, at present."

"On these terms, I will not receive you. You can make the experiment for twelve months; and then, if you think you can subscribe to the requirement, you can come forward for full admission into the work."

The candidate paused again, looked mortified, and then said resolutely, "Well, then, sir, I solemnly promise to give it up."

"Forever?"

"Yes, by the help of God, not to resume it."

On another occasion, when holding the same responsible station, the doctor made much shorter work with a candidate. Addressing the young man, he asked,—

"Do you take tobacco in any form, brother?"

"I take a little snuff, sir."

"Give it up?"

"I will give it up, sir, if the conference require me."

"I am the conference, sir, while I am seated here, and I order you to give it up."

The candidate here extended toward the

president, a small box about the size of the first joint of his thumb, saying, "That, sir, serves me some months."

"Well," answered the doctor, "hand it this way; it is so *small* it can be no great cross to give it up."

Toward the close of the year 1814, the Missionary Society of the Wesleyan Connection was formed. Previously to this period, Dr. Coke, an early co-adjutor of Wesley, had, in himself, been a virtual missionary society. He had projected missions, raised the supplies by his eloquent appeals to the members of the societies, directed the labours of the missionarries, and gone with them to share their privations. But it pleased the Great Head of the Church that his devoted servant should, while on his way to Ceylon, to form new missions, sleep in the depths of the ocean. As Coke was to the Wesleyan Missions what Wesley was to the connection generally, when he died the work he performed was assumed by the whole body. Dr. Clarke was present and preached a stirring sermon at the City Road Chapel, London, on the occasion of the formation of the society, and was subsequently a prominent instrument in making it what it is now, the contributor of a half a million of dollars annually, for the extension of the gospel in heathen lands. He added to the labours already mentioned, frequent occasional sermons in different parts of the kingdom, in behalf of missions. We shall hear of him on such occasions, preaching to audiences which crowd to their utmost capacity the chapels, and obtaining unaccustomed collections by his eloquent appeals. From this period, calls to "open chapels," to deliver charity sermons, and to aid the collections of various financial projects connected with religion, drew more and more upon his time and strength. Sometimes, advantage was taken of the large audiences which his popularity drew together, to put forward, unexpectedly to the people, the claims of some benevolent enterprise. This considerably annoyed the doctor.

On one occasion an admission fee was required of his audience, for some charity. When about half way through his sermon, having made an occasion for speaking of the poor, he paused, looked toward the part of the house where they usually sat, and said, sharply, "I see you have contrived to keep the poor away. If you do not desist from the practice, Adam Clarke will enter your chapel no more."

His missionary services and duties during the years he was president of the conference, occasioned frequent tours into various parts of England and Ireland. In visiting the latter country, he looked once more upon the scene of his early days. The companions of his youth were nearly all gone.

Entering the burial-place adjacent to the old church, he remarked: "Here lie several of my

The Ruins of the Old Church in which Dr. Clarke was educated.—p. 162.

ancestors and I go to lie most probably in another land, and shall not, in all likelihood, be gathered to my fathers; but I shall be found when all the quick and the dead shall stand before the Lord; and wheresoever my dust shall be scattered, the voice of the Lord shall call it together, and I shall stand in my lot, at the end of days. May I then be found of him in peace, without spot and without blame, and have an entrance into the holiest through the blood of Jesus."

We have thus, in sketching the history of Dr. Clarke's abundant labours, noticed his connection with the Bible Society, "The Record Commission," the Commentary, occasional publications, and the special duties belonging to the presidency of the conference. It will be recollected that he filled his appointments during this period as a circuit preacher, ministering to large audiences every Sabbath, and frequently during week evenings. As intimated, we have anticipated in this chapter the *close* of the "Record" labours which extended to 1819—and also the completion of the Commentary in 1826. We have now arrived at the year 1815—at which time he was fifty-five years of age.

CHAPTER XV.

RETIRED, BUT NOT RESTING.

Resolves to leave London—Removes to Millbrook—Cultivates his land—Kindness to animals—A petted donkey—The painted cross—His evenings at Millbrook—A chapel for the poor—A Sunday-school—Causes of the attendance of the poor—Dr. Clarke's daughters become colporteurs—The poor sailors "warmed and clothed"—Dr. Clarke and his wife's shopping money—The coronation honoured—Two high-priests of Budhoo—The occasion of their voyage to England—Placed under the instruction of Dr. Clarke—Their instruction—Their surprise at seeing snow and ice—They are baptized, and admitted to the Christian Church—Their return to Ceylon—A letter from the son of the elder priest—Dr. Clarke a third time President of the Conference.

TOWARD the close of the year 1815, Dr. Clarke decided to remove from London. Some parts of his Commentary were passing through the press, and the labour of completing the manuscript pressed upon him daily. In this great thoroughfare of business and travel, he was subject to constant interruptions. Besides, the friction of fifty-five years upon his physical frame, although it had not taken all his energy, had abated the vigour of earlier manhood. He says; "I have made up my mind to leave this distracting place; to get out of the way of even a turnpike road, that I may get as much out of every passing hour as I can. I ought to have no work at present but the Commentary; for none can comprehend the trouble, and often anguish, which the writing of the notes cost me; and what adds to the perplexity is, the multitude of little things to which, almost incessantly, my attention is demanded; and to which, while remaining in town, I must attend."

Having, therefore, resolved to leave the city, he purchased a small estate a few miles from Liverpool, to which he removed with his family on the 20th of September, 1815. The conference, recognising the importance of his engagements with the Record Commission and the Commentary, connected his name with the Manchester circuit, to which he was to go once a month, leaving the rest of the time at his own disposal.

To his new residence he gave the name of Millbrook. An important object to be secured now, was a healthy stimulus to his mind and body. To obtain this, he spent considerable time in labour upon his land. True to his characteristics, he began to apply his scientific knowledge to the improvement of its husbandry. Soon its exhausted soil began to yield an unusual crop. His domestic animals received his special attention. With his own hand he fed them, and showed them that tender care which even a brute understands. To carry out this feeling, he purchased an ass, with the professed object of trying the power of kindness on his proverbially perverse temper. He gave him the name of Baudet, and set apart an enclosure for his especial use, sufficiently large to satisfy his love of liberty. Here Baudet was fed, petted, and flattered into good humour with himself and the world in general. We are not sure that there was in this treatment much of a trial of his amiability. Most donkeys would be good-natured when having things their own way. The heavy burden and the long journey try the temper. But, however, the doctor's object was accomplished, in showing that even an ass will be moved by love, for Baudet manifested for him the docility and fondness of a spaniel.

But let us step into the house, now that he is well settled in his new home. It is evening. The children are now young men and women, and some of them have left the parental roof to assume the responsibilities of life. Still there is a large family circle. As the doctor's time is so much at his command, he confines his studies mostly to the light of the day —rising early, as he has always done from childhood. The evenings are spent with his family. The scholar, who has passed the day in hard thinking, is now the free, light-hearted parent and husband. Mrs. Clarke, who, the doctor says, "is one of the best readers I ever heard, and can read aloud three hours together," entertains the domestic circle with a book. Her husband, whose varied and almost exhaustless store of knowledge enables him to speak freely on the subject which is read, criticises the facts, or discusses the views of the author. He enters into this entertainment with freshness of feeling and readiness of utterance. His vivacity is contagious, and all are interested and instructed. The exercise is not a task, but a privilege to be enjoyed.

Not unfrequently we shall find the doctor and his wife differently employed. He has brought the manuscript of his Commentary from his study, which he has written during the day. He is reading it to Mrs. Clarke, to whose judgment of its sentiments and mode of expression he pays great respect.

The neighbourhood of Millbrook was mostly Roman Catholic, and was constituted generally of the poor. There was no Protestant preaching place within several miles. To supply this deficiency, Dr. Clarke built a chapel near his house, and at his own expense, sufficiently large to hold three hundred persons. The pulpit was supplied, with his assistance, by the preachers of the neighbouring circuit. The poor were invited to come freely. They had said, "If you had a chapel, we would all go your road." A Sunday-school of forty scholars was at once established. Into this the doctor went often, speaking kindly and familiarly to the children, and making suggestions concerning the regulations of the school. The Roman Catholic children were, at first, timid and distant. A few came to the school, and went away to their own chapel when the preaching commenced. Soon, (through the children in part,) the parents became interested, ventured to hear the word from Protestant lips, and remained to weep—to pray, and rejoice in salvation through Christ Jesus alone. But there were causes at work to draw them to evangelical preaching—Christian in their character, and, therefore, worthy to be maintained and imitated. The following are illustrations. The poor labourers of the vicinity had been required by their employer to commence work at an unusually early hour, and expressed their fear lest they should not awake early enough.

"Leave that to me," said the doctor. "I am always up in season."

"The next morning, precisely at four o'clock, the doctor was unexpectedly at the doors of the poor men in his neighbourhood, rousing them from their slumber—a practice he continued for some time."

His daughters, fully sympathizing with their father's benevolent feelings, went from house to house, scattering tracts, bearing his contributions of food and clothing for the destitute, praying with the sick, and inviting all to Christ. The consequence was, a chapel full of attentive hearers, and the conversion of many souls.

We need not say, after the statement of the

above facts, that the children loved Dr. Clarke. The children of his vicinity having heard him say that he was very fond of an apple while the dew of the morning rested upon it—an expression which may have meant more than they understood—rose early the next morning, and, selecting some apples from the trees moist with the dew, and, gently tapping upon his study window, presented the offering, and scampered off with glad hearts.

During the winter following his removal to Millbrook, Dr. Clarke had a special occasion for the exercise of his benevolence. The cold was unusually severe. The seamen of Liverpool were, in great numbers, thrown out of employment, and made dependent upon charity for support. Dr. Clarke invited twenty of these poor fellows to Millbrook, and opened for them some untenanted cottages on his place. Not being able to supply them with beds, a plenty of clean straw was procured, and an abundance of blankets purchased, so that they were made entirely comfortable. At appointed times they assembled in his kitchen for their meals, one in turn remaining to cook for the rest. During the working hours they were employed on the farm in such work as they could conveniently do, it being a maxim with the doctor to encourage industry in all about him. Thus, for several weeks, were they supported, until the season enabled them to obtain employment.

But his exertions did not stop here. He used his extensive influence with the wealthy and honoured to provoke them to labours of love for the suffering. We will present two more brief illustrations of his benevolence, and pass on to other matters.

His wife had entrusted him with a considerable sum of money, for divers small purchases, as he was leaving home for Manchester. While in the city, some of his countrymen assailed him with their tales of sufferings. He never went shielded against such attacks, and their complaints were too touching for him to resist. He emptied his purse into their hats, and returned without the desired articles. The doctor says: "I had to answer for it. 'Well, Mary, dear,' I said, 'I did not spend it for myself.' "

In 1821, on the occasion of the coronation of George IV., as King of England, the doctor honoured the event by making the poor happy. The story is best told by himself, in a letter to his sons—

"Dear Lads:—We have had a great feast on the occasion of the coronation. We brought all our tenants together, even to the least of their young children, and gave them a dinner. They ate a world of beef, pies, puddings, and cheese, besides half a bushel of currants and cherries. To all our people I also gave a holiday, and paid each his day's wages; and when all was over, I gave every child a penny; all above eight years old a sixpence, and to every grown person a shilling. We sang and prayed, and afterward, I dismissed them. They were as happy as they could be."

In the year 1818, Dr. Clarke received into his family at Millbrook two high-priests of Budhoo, from the island of Ceylon. The history of their connection with him, and subsequent conversion and return to their native country, is given, in the sources of information before us, in detail, and is very interesting. We will give it as briefly as is consistent with a clear presentation of its prominent features.

The English missionaries at Ceylon had translated the New Testament into the dialect of that island. These two priests, while offering daily sacrifices to their idols, had read a copy of this translation. They became deeply interested, especially in the sufferings and death of Christ. The more they read, the more they wished to know; and they determined to visit England, the source, they thought, of information of a religion so wonderful. The doctor, true to his principles of Christian benevolence, consented to take them into his family, and instruct them gratuitously; the Wesleyan Missionary Society agreeing to be at the expense of their support. They were cousins; the older (Munhi Rat'hana, Teerunanxi,) twenty-seven years of age, and the younger (Dherma Rama,) about twenty-five.

They had been in the priesthood more than six years.

Their instruction required great patience and wisdom. Old prejudices had to be destroyed, and the foundation laid in their minds for the first principles of Christianity. They questioned every step of this process. Early in the morning they were found in their instructor's study, listening to his patient teaching. The story of the cross melted them to tears; but they were greatly astonished that Christ should have such amazing power to work miracles, and yet be an unresisting sufferer in the hands of his enemies. They had many doubts to be removed, and they were long in receiving the great doctrines of the cross; for to them, most emphatically, "Great was the mystery of godliness."

Their improvement in their English studies was very rapid. Dr. Clarke performed many experiments for them in natural philosophy and chemistry. They earnestly inquired for the facts, and when they saw them developed, and beautifully set forth in the experiments, their joy was expressed in the warmest manner.

Having lived in a warm climate, as the winter approached, their curiosity was greatly excited by the novel appearance of nature. They had heard of "solid water," and frost and snow, but regarded the stories concerning them to be the fables of travellers. Their emotions, on being introduced to the marvels of an English winter, are thus described by an eye-witness:—

"It happened in the winter of this year that the first snow fell in the night, and in great abundance; their bed-room looked into the garden, and when they rose in the morning, and drew up the curtain as usual to look out, their surprise was uncontrollable, and amounted to a sensation of fear when they beheld the wide white world before them. In amazement, they ran into the study, and thence with Dr. Clarke into the garden, to see and handle this wonderful phenomenon; and when they felt it beneath their feet, and caught its rapidly dissolving particles in their hands, their surprise yielded to their pleasure, and it was with difficulty they could be restrained from exposing their uninured bodies to the severities of an English winter's day. Not long after this the fish-pond was so completely and solidly frozen, that they were taken to behold, what they had so long wished to see, the "solid water;" but its smooth surface retained too much of its old appearance to quell their fears and satisfy their doubts. Dr. Clarke then got on it, and walked to the middle of it, but still they had so much faith in him that, though they thought he might do thus much, they were not sure they could do so unhurt, until they were further assured by seeing other members of the family—females and all—follow his example. Dr. Clarke's nephew, having put on his skates, began to pass over the surface with a motion which seemed to them like flying; but perceiving him to be every where in contact with the mass, their doubt then gave way to ecstacy, and they too walked on the "solid water," not only with delight but amusement. They would then have a piece of it, which, on account of its thickness, it was a matter of difficulty to obtain, and were not contented until they had, by the action of fire, themselves reduced it once more to its usual appearance. Thus were they taught and pleased, and certainly benefited by the varied instructions they received."

After Dr. Clarke had carefully taught them for twenty-two months, and had faithfully inquired respecting the grounds of their profession of saving faith in Christ, they were baptized by him in Liverpool, admitted into the Christian Church and to the sacrament of the Lord's supper. Up to this time, Dherma had "been in bondage through the fear of death;" but, on retiring from this solemn service, he exclaimed, joyfully, "Oh, now I no fear to die. If I die I go straight to the kingdom of God." Munhi, on returning to his room, prostrated himself on the floor, and spent a long time in tears, and prayer, and praise. The former took the name of Alexander, for Sir Alexander Johnstone, his friend, in whose company they had come from India, and the latter that of his instructor, Adam. Soon after this interesting event, they returned, with many expressions of gratitude to Dr. Clarke, to their native country; where, amidst the wickedness of heathenism, they ever remained true to their Christian profession. They wrote several touching letters to their much-loved instructor, while on their way to Ceylon, and after they arrived there. A letter from a *son* of Munhi, written to a member of Dr. Clarke's family, fifteen years after the doctor's death, will give, as a closing item in this account, interesting proof of some of the later fruits of the conversion of these Budhists. It is dated Ceylon, March 20th, 1847.

"My dear father told me you would be a friend to me if I wrote to you after his death. After labouring in his Saviour's service for many years, he expired on the 13th of November, 1840, in a sure hope of a resurrection to eternal life. My dear father taught me to pray, like Dr. Clarke taught him to pray, who had put over his bed, while he was at Millbrook, in Singhalese and English, '*Munhi, forget not to pray!*' So I am praying to my great and good God, for myself and for you. I want English teaching. My father told me when he was dying, 'Write to ——, and that lady will help you to English teaching.' I never saw Alexander Dherma Rhama, my father's companion, but I wrote to inform him of my father's death, and from his answer to my letter, I learn that he is the head man over the people of the village of Moratova, twenty-four miles from Galle. *He is yet sure in the Christian faith.* I have but one sister: her name is Elizabeth. I am fifteen; and my ruling passion is to come to England, get English teaching, and see that blessed country."

What a beautiful illustration is this whole account of the Budhist priests of the power of the gospel over heathen minds!

In July, of the year 1822, Dr. Clarke was for the third time elected president of the Wesleyan Conference, an honour, as we have said, never before bestowed so often upon any one individual.

Dr. Clarke's Residence.

p. 177.

CHAPTER XVI.

THE PALACE OF THE GREAT, AND THE COTTAGE OF THE POOR.

Dr. Clarke settles in Eastcot—Temporary chapel—Sunday-school—The new chapel—The duke of Sussex—The duke's Bibliographical library—He invites Dr. Clarke to visit him—The visit—A second visit to the duke—The duke returns the visits of Dr. Clarke—The levee—Dr. Clarke's acquaintance with English bishops—A liberal neighbour—Watch-Night.

EARLY in the year 1824, Dr. Clarke removed to London from Millbrook, having sold his estate there. He was led to this step by the fact that most of his children were residing in the city. But the noise and the many interruptions of the great metropolis were less than ever congenial with his feelings since he had experienced the pleasures of his retirement at Millbrook. Consequently, he purchased a situation, in the fall of the same year, in Eastcott, about sixteen miles from London. Amidst the rural scenery of Hayden Hall, as he named his residence, we shall now further follow his history, and study his character.

One of his first acts, after his removal, was to provide the preaching of the word of life for the poor of the neighbourhood. There being no house of worship near, at first, an old coach-house and a stable were cleared, and provided with rough seats for the use of the preachers. He preached the opening sermon, setting forth the object of the house of worship, which was, he told them, to hold up, through the ministry, Christ and the cross, and to gather the children into the Sunday-school. All were invited to come freely. After the sermon, one of the doctor's friends went from house to house, and obtained the names of seventy children pledged to attend the school. This place of worship was soon found to be too small; a more commodious chapel was consequently erected. How natural, even in our day, do the following remarks sound, which were made by Dr. Clarke after the Sunday-school was organized in the new house:—"Well, now I want books; I have got but twenty-four 'Spelling Books,' and what are these among so many? Testaments I also require. Some of my friends have done enough—we can do no more—yet books we want, and books we must have. There are some young people coming, seventeen and eighteen years of age, who cannot read a letter, and yet desire to learn. Some of the children would be glad of some hymn books, too; we shall shortly have the songs of Zion here. Hallelujah!"

How great a blessing would have been the publications of our Sunday-school Union in such a crisis! These lights to the path of the rising generation had not then dawned upon the church.

Passing from the home and neighbourhood of the doctor, let us follow him awhile in his intercourse with the learned and distinguished.

We cannot detail the interesting history of the first introduction of Dr. Clarke to the Duke of Sussex, brother to the then reigning king, George IV. The occasion of their acquaintance and subsequent intimacy, was their mutual interest in the study of the Bible. The duke was a distinguished Biblical scholar. In his library were fifteen hundred copies of the Bible, in all languages and editions, the most perfect collection, perhaps, in the world, costing more than $200,000. When sixty-five years of age, he had spent thirty-five of them in feeble health. He remarked at one time to his friend, Dr. Clarke, that he had been accustomed, during this painful experience, to read the Bible alone, every morning, two hours before breakfast. The reader will be interested to view Dr. Clarke, for a short time, in his intercourse with such a man. We have grouped the several occasions together, though they a little preceded or succeeded the present point of our narrative.

The private secretary of the duke having had occasion, in the year 1822, to write to Dr. Clarke with regard to a matter of literary interest, appended the following note:—"The duke commands me to say, that he trusts whenever you come to London, you will honour him with a visit: when he will be proud to show you his library, and be most happy to make the acquaintance of a man of whose talents and character he has so exalted an opinion."

In May following, Dr. Clarke being in London, he was invited to dine with the duke. The doctor went, and was received by his royal friend in his private room, and was conducted by him through his library, shown many curious things, and asked bibliographical questions. The doctor's answers the duke requested his librarian to note, as "curious and important." After dining with the duke, and many distinguished friends, the doctor intimated his intention of retiring. But he was requested to remain till all the company had departed. Dr. Clarke closes his account of the visit, in a letter to his daughter, by adding:—"When they were all gone, the duke sat down on his sofa, and beckoned me to come and sit down beside him, on his right hand; and he entered for a considerable time, into a most familiar conversation with me. At last, a servant in the royal livery came to me, saying:—'Sir, the carriage is in waiting.' I rose up, and his royal highness rose at the same time, took me affectionately by the hand, told me I must come and visit him some morning when he was alone, which time should be arranged between me and his secretary,—

bade me a friendly good-night; and I was then conducted by the servant to the door of the palace, when lo, and behold! one of the royal carriages was in waiting to carry a Methodist preacher, your old weather-beaten father, to his own lodgings!"

In April, 1825, the doctor was again invited, together with his son, to visit Kensington Palace. He received a note from the secretary, saying that the duke was anxious to introduce him to a very enlightened nobleman, the Duke of Hamilton. The visit we will let the doctor describe, reminding the reader that he was writing to a member of his family, and not for the public eye. On his arrival, he says:—

"The Duke of Sussex soon made his appearance, for by this time the whole company were in the pavilion, and singling me out, took me by the hand, and led me forward to two Indian gentlemen, saying, 'Here is my friend, Dr. Adam Clarke, who will speak Persian or Arabic with any of you.' I turned, and taking John by the arm, said:—'May it please your royal highness, I have the honour of presenting to you my eldest son.' He took him by the hand, and bade him welcome, and on the arrival of any new guest, introduced both myself and my son."

A few months after this occasion, the Duke of Sussex returned Dr. Clarke's visit. He came to Hayden Hall without parade, as a private gentleman, and was received by the doctor in that polite but plain manner which became his position and his profession. After dining, the royal visitor entered the library and museum of his friend, and was entertained until a late hour there, by the stores of Biblical and other curiosities, which the doctor had accumulated through a public life of nearly half a century.

In October, of the succeeding year, the duke repeated his visit, dining at Hayden Hall, and discussing the character and history of ancient Hebrew manuscripts in the possession of Dr. Clarke, with all the enthusiasm of a genuine lover of the pure Word of God. To the end of the doctor's life this intimacy continued, by interchange of visits, and by letters on learned matters of mutual interest. The Commentary, in which his royal highness took a deep interest, was several times the occasion of correspondence.

By some of the distinguished bishops of the Church of England Dr. Clarke's acquaintance was sought, on terms of considerable intimacy. On one occasion, having just returned from a call upon the bishop of London, he remarked to a friend, pleasantly, "Yes, I have been with the bishop; but it was not for my son, recollect; I shall not ask, in this way, a favour at any man's hands." This son, to whom he refers, became one of the chaplains to the Duke of Sussex.

Turning from these scenes of flattering attention, we find Dr. Clarke again in the humble dwellings of the poor. The winter of 1829–30 was one of great severity. Many families of his own neighbourhood were insufficiently clothed and scantily fed. Dr. Clarke employed one of his old domestics to go into every house, and inquire concerning their wants. Then with his own hand did the doctor supply their lack of necessary food and clothing, until his means were exhausted. With a heart still pained at the suffering yet unalleviated, he was pondering what next he could do, when one of his wealthy neighbours gave him a handsome sum to distribute, with which he at once went to London, and purchased flannels, blankets, calicoes, and other necessary articles. With these treasures he hastened back to Eastcot, and spent three days in distributing them to the most necessitous.

In the spirit of such labour, Dr. Clarke commenced the new year. He says, in a letter to his daughter: "Most of our people went to the chapel last evening, to hold a watch-night. Mother was not well enough to watch in the new year, so I kept watch by myself in the parlour, and was in solemn prayer for you *all*, when the clock struck twelve, and for some time after. Even to watch by myself I found to be a good thing; I felt that it might be the last watch-night I might ever celebrate. Mary, dear, pray much to God, and make him your portion. I remained up till the preacher and our people returned from the chapel. I had an excellent fire, and a good supper for them; I made them sit down while I served them myself; they were pleased, and thus we were all pleased."

CHAPTER XVII.

AN APPROPRIATE, LAST LABOUR

Shetland Islands—A mission to them begun—Dr. Clarke has the responsibility for it—A tour in behalf of Shetland—A noble donor—Tracts for "Good Little Girls"—A visit to the Shetland Islands—Dr. Clarke's solicitude for Shetland—Irish free schools—The first school—A new difficulty—Encouraging results—Dr. Clarke's visit to Ireland—Sunday-schools—Plan of proceeding—A second visit to the Irish schools.

THE last labours of Dr. Clarke for the cause of Christ extend from the year 1822 to the close of his life in 1832. They consisted almost wholly in efforts to open new fields of missionary enterprise, and the establishment—in the neglected districts of his native country, Ireland—of day and Sunday-schools for the poor.

At the conference, in 1822, Dr. Clarke's attention was directed to the moral condition of the Shetland Islands, lying a short distance from the northern portion of Scotland. The conference missionary funds not allowing the establishment of missions immediately in this direction, on the credit of the treasury, Dr. Clarke began by making applications to a few benevolent persons of his acquaintance for contributions to commence the enterprise. His old friend and coadjutor in every good work, Robert Scott, Esq., with his family, gave the work a start by the ready offering of $600, and a pledge from Mrs. Scott of $50 toward every chapel which should be built in the progress of the mission. Thus encouraged, the missionary committee appointed two young men as missionaries, and sent them to Dr. Clarke for instructions.

The young men immediately repaired to Dr. Clarke's residence, received his suggestions, and then proceeded to their appointed work. They were at once successful. The islanders, 25,000 in number, were, in many parts, wholly destitute of ministerial labour, and in others only occasionally visited by clergymen from Scotland. The want of chapels, as the cold weather approached, was severely felt. Dr. Clarke had directed the missionaries to contract no debts, for any purpose. Therefore the money for the support of the preachers and the erection of places of worship, must be procured by himself. He immediately commenced a begging tour. He preached, and among the multitudes which ever flocked to his ministry, he took collections, made private appeals to the rich, and solicited contributions of the products of their business from the manufacturer and mechanic, until he himself was astonished at the greatness of the work which increased upon his hands. He closes one of his letters to the missionaries with the following words: "Tell me all that concerns yourselves and the work. Be steady,—act by united counsels,—love one another,—help each other,—speak well of each other,—prefer one another in love. Act as evangelists,—preach Jesus—Jesus, in the plenitude of his salvation;" and he adds, "I have sent off to you about six thousand tracts and pamphlets, and I will, if God spare me, see you in the spring."

The demands of the mission pressing upon him at one time beyond his collections, he says, "I prayed, called earnestly upon God, and sat down and wept till I could scarcely see to write or read." He appealed in this crisis to his friends, Mr. and Mrs. Scott. Dr. Clarke then writes: "They came, and I set off in my bad health to London to meet them; and oh, what a meeting! Their hearts were nearly as full as mine. Says Mr. Scott, 'Come, let me have a check; I will give orders on my bank for $500.' Says Mrs. Scott, 'and I will give $25.' 'And I am desired,' says Mr. Scott, 'by my sister-in-law, Miss Grainger, to give $25, and, lest any chapel begun should be impeded, here is $50 more, and thus I will give the check for $600. And this is not all that I will do. I tell you again, I will give $50 to every house or chapel begun under your direction in Shetland.' " Dr. Clarke then adds, "I thanked God,—I thanked them; and could have kissed the ground on which they trod. I said in my heart, 'O my poor Shetlanders, (whom I have never seen, and now never shall, but God has laid them upon my heart,) God has not forgotten you.' "

In a note, appended to a letter to the mis sionaries about this time, he says: "A little half-granddaughter of mine (Caroline Smith) is just now dead,—ten years old, and has left a most glorious testimony for God. It is now in the press, and I will send some for presents to good little girls in Shetland."

Notwithstanding the fear expressed above, by Dr. Clarke, that he should never see his Shetlanders, he did visit them, with several friends of the mission, in 1826, and again in 1828. His detailed account of these visits is full of interest, and exhibits Dr. Clarke's characteristic trait of close observation of all which was around him, and his ability to gather rich treasures of knowledge from every source.

These mission stations continued to strengthen and multiply, until they became an established portion of the Wesleyan missionary fields. As late as 1831, (about one year before the Doctor's death,) when the burden of them was still pressing upon him, and when the toils of seventy-one years had caused him to anticipate the close of his earthly sojourning, he bids the Shetlanders adieu in the following strain:

"Poor Shetland! I have worked hard for thee; many a quire,—many a ream of paper have I written to describe thy wants, and to beg for supplies; and several thousands of miles have I travelled, in order to raise those supplies which by letter I had solicited for thee! It is now 'almost done, and almost over.' May God raise thee up another friend, that will be, if possible, more earnest and faithful, and at the same time more successful! And now, I must say, may the *Holy Trinity* be thy incessant friend, oh, my poor Shetland!"

The burden of this mission had not been removed from Dr. Clarke, when a friend, who was preaching through the district of country in Ireland where Dr. Clarke had preached in his youth, desired him to do for the neglected children of Ireland what he had done for the people of Shetland. His purpose to accept of this new labour of love being known, several individuals of wealth offered to be responsible for the expense of such free schools as should be formed under his supervision. Having made careful inquiry, the field of operations was located in the province of Ulster, in the north of Ireland. He found this section of the country destitute of schools, and of any associations, either religious or benevolent.

The population was composed of both Catholics and Protestants. The Port Rush district was selected in which to make the first experiment. A missionary was sent through it, to inquire if the people would have a free school on week days, in which their children should be taught to read; and Sunday-schools, in which they might learn the way to heaven. At once the country was awake on the subject. They all said, "Yes, let Dr. Clarke send us teachers."

Having with great care obtained men of good English education and of tried piety for teachers, and having written out a simple plan by which the scholars should be received and instructed, and furnished money for the preparatory expenses, Dr. Clarke requested that the work should be at once commenced. The people rallied in great numbers at a place appointed, when a new difficulty was presented. It was expected that the private houses of the poor people themselves would be sufficiently large for school-rooms, but no such house being found, and not being willing to lose the present opportunity, the parents proposed to occupy a sand-pit, though they were already in the piercing cold of December. A gentleman who lived near, seeing the zeal of the people, and knowing the sand-pit to be wholly unsuitable, offered his parlour to the teacher until a more proper room could be obtained. The teacher, out of school-hours, went among the parents, reading to them the Scriptures, praying with them, and exhorting them to flee from the wrath to come. This was indeed a new thing, and many of the poor people, who had scarcely ever heard any sort of prayer, now learned themselves to pray. The numbers of the school increased so rapidly, that in two months the parlour became entirely too small. A house in the neighbourhood was hired, and a hundred children, from four to fourteen years of age, were made happy in gleaning the rudiments of an education. So wicked had been the habits of these children, that but few of them could give a simple answer of yes or no, without taking the name of God in vain. The gentleman whose parlour was occupied, informed Dr. Clarke, only about two months after the schools were established, that before the teacher came, the children, with their noisy and wicked conduct, were not only a nuisance, but a curse. The peaceable people were obliged to drive them off from depredations, by whips and sticks; and that now their voice is not to be heard in the streets, and that order and decorum universally prevail.

In the spring following the beginning of this good work, Dr. Clarke set out on a visit of inspection to the Irish schools, carrying with him several teachers, for the purpose of ascertaining himself, the best locations and opening new schools, as well as examining those already in operation. He says, "The poor people, both Popish and Protestant, were, like true sons of Erin—red hot—made glad—to hear that their children might, without money and without price, be taught to read, spell and write their own names; and where they at last found that there was neither religion, devotion, nor common sense in sheer ignorance." He studiously avoided giving any denominational character to the religious instruction in these schools, but made it an indispensable condition every where, that the Old and New Testaments should be read in them, disapproving in strong terms of the government plan of leaving the Bible out of the schools. Every where he made the Sunday-school an attendant upon the week-day school. The parents as well as children, including even many of the Roman Catholic population, flocked to these. The great difficulty he had to meet, in this part of the work, was the lack of suitable teachers, as but few were capable of teaching. Upon the instructor of the week-day school came most of the Sabbath-school labour at first, but soon pious persons were raised up to supply this deficiency.

His plan of opening a new school is thus described. "The day previously to that appointed for the purpose, the children get warning of it, and the parents and children assemble, sometimes in a barn, or, if fine weather, in the open air, under the shelter of a hawthorn hedge. The intense interest of all on these occasions is wonderful, and the gentry offered with zeal and rivalship, land or houses on their estates, in the recesses of the bogs and mountains scarcely, indeed, accessible, owing to the bad roads, but still swarming with a vast population of children, who, on announcement, came pouring down the hills; the parents were all on my right hand, the children on the left, and I gave them an impressive address for half an hour: at the close, sung and prayed with and for them.

The following description, illustrating his mode of proceeding, is quite life-like:—

"We set off for a place called Croagh, where the whole youth of a large and populous district, have long been and still are without education, for there is no school existing of any kind for many miles. It was published in the county that I was expected there this day in order to form a school. When we got within a mile of the place, we saw several squads of children, with their mothers, coming down the hills and over the moors, from all quarters, from a mile and a half to two miles, to the school house, which is little more than half finished, and which is to serve as a centre for the conglomeration of these various masses. As we could not go into this half built house, we were told that a farmer had prepared a small barn, which was about half a mile off; I then proclaimed an adjournment to the barn, and setting off myself, they all filed after me, both the children and their mothers, my companions bringing up the rear. When I arrived at the place, I addressed the parents out of doors, and laid down the general rules and conditions on which the children were to be admitted, and on which they were to be continued in the school. I then, standing at the barn door, admitted them one by one into the place to the number of 133;—introduced the school-master to the general assembly;—gave his character and qualifications;—specified what sort of teaching the children were to receive;—the discipline under which they were to be brought; how they were to learn their duty to God, to their parents, and to each other;—how to pray to avoid every evil in word and deed, in spirit, temper, and desire; to be industrious, cleanly and orderly; respectful to their superiors, affectionate to their relations, kind and obliging to their equals. After a good deal of exhortation, I then proceeded to bring the children out of the barn, laying my hands upon their heads, and praying to God for his blessing upon them all, delivered them again to their parents, to be brought back on the morrow in order to be registered in the school, classified, &c.—The children were, on the whole, really a fine progeny; males and females, from fourteen to four years of age."

In the following year, Dr. Clarke again visited his schools, then greatly increased in number, in scholars, and in influence. But a serious illness, while in Ireland, preventing a personal examination of them all, he was obliged to be content with the report of their teachers. The rude but heart-felt tribute of respect which these neglected children of poverty rendered to their benefactor afforded him nobler satisfaction than Napoleon ever felt when returning from the conquest of nations. Under God, Dr. Clarke had conquered ignorance and driven moral darkness from many hearts. Where he had been, cleanliness, good order, and, in many cases, religious peace, followed.

These schools, the Sunday as well as the week-day schools, were without any sectarian character, and the doctor was, without a penny for his services, the agent for the benevolence of a few individuals. After his death the Wesleyan Missionary Society took them, at the request of his friends, under their care, and continued them much in the same spirit with which they had been begun. We may remark here, in anticipation of the account of Doctor Clarke's death, that he died with his hand to this work for the children of his native country. Were it not for extending too far this narrative, we could give still more evidence that none of the abundant and varied labour of his life gave him more satisfaction than this.

Connected with the Shetland and school labour in point of time, is Dr. Clarke's revision of his Commentary, for a new edition. "The author's own and last hand" was put to this entire work, a few months before his death, and before his last visit to his schools. The copyright of the Commentary thus revised, after having disposed of large former editions, he sold for nine thousand dollars.

CHAPTER XVIII.

A MORE FAMILIAR ACQUAINTANCE.

Dr. Clarke's personal appearance—His scholarship—His memory—His library of printed books: their value—His manuscript library: its value—The museum—Dr. Clarke's travelling library—The means by which his library and museum were obtained—Dr. Clarke's frequent preaching—His character as a preacher—His popularity—The relation of his study of the Bible to his preaching—Habits of preparation for the pulpit—Manner of handling his texts—The great secret of his pulpit power—His favourite themes in the pulpit—His manner in preaching—Dr. Clarke's habitual kindness—A happy turn of an awkward incident—The young lady and the roasted potato—Feeling towards friends—Love for children—Letter to a grandson—Dr. Clarke's pleasantry—His wife could keep a secret—The secret of Dr. Clarke's success—His industry—Eminent testimonies of his industry—His promptness—An anecdote illustrating it—His love of order illustrated—Early rising enforced—An anecdote—Dr. Clarke's example may be imitated.

ADAM CLARKE, in person, was about five feet nine inches high, and, in the latter years of his life, rather corpulent,—his hair of venerable whiteness, brushed back from his forehead,—his complexion ruddy, his countenance open, his form erect, and step firm. His dress was always well adjusted and neat. The black suit usually worn by clergymen did not agree well, he thought, with the cheerful character of the gospel of which they were ministers. He generally appeared in public in the dress of an English country gentleman, with top-boots, drab breeches, blue coat, with covered or silk buttons, pale buff vest, drab hat, and white neckcloth.

We shall not attempt to decide the question of the character of his scholarship. We have presented the facts of his connection with the ripest scholars of his age, not as a passing acquaintance, but as an associate, a co-labourer—honoured and respected by them through many years. These, and other facts which we have detailed, must settle the question, in the minds of candid men, of his scholarship. That he was profound in all the departments of learning with which he was acquainted, is more than the most partial friendship can claim for him. He did, indeed, "intermeddle with all wisdom." That which he once learned, he never forgot. He had a most remarkable memory. He could, at any time, recall the sentiment of any author in his very extensive range of reading; and, so exact were his habits of order, and so well arranged was every thing in his own mind, that he could tell in what connection these sentiments stood, and would often go to his library, and take down at once the book in which they were contained, and turn to the page on which they were found.

But the most remarkable feature of his intellectual character was, the power to use the results of his varied study, without apparent exertion, in the practical duties of the ministry—both in what he spoke and wrote for the good of men. It came at his bidding so readily, and fitted into its place so naturally, that it was useful to the learned and unlearned.

His library of printed works was set up in five rooms, and included about ten thousand volumes. Here were the best editions of the classic authors of Greece and Rome, valuable standard works in a great variety of languages, but especially the pure word of God, and whatever might illustrate its pages, of criticism or history. This part of his library was valued at $15,000.* The manuscript library was one of the most extensive private collections in the world, and was valued at about $8000. Some of the manuscripts dated as early as A. D. 1024,

* The printed books actually brought, after the doctor's decease, in an auction sale of ten days' continuance, £3,200, and the manuscripts £180 more, making the considerable sum of £5000, or not far from $23,000. We are safe in estimating the value of the library and museum at $25,000. Some of the books and manuscripts sold for more and some for less than their value: the following were among the former class, we should think:—A famous manuscript Bible, translated into the English language, by Wiclif, in two volumes, brought £100; Biblia Sacra Polyglotta, £57; a copy of the first complete edition of the English Bible, by Coverdale, £63; a copy of Erasmus' New Testament, which cost the doctor one shilling, brought £10 15s.

and but few as late as the eighteenth century. In the museum, were to be found curiosities from ancient Greece and Rome, including coins, monuments and mosaics—Indian, Burmese, Egyptian and Chinese idols,—medals,—several fac similes of ancient charters, maps and charts, and a valuable collection of minerals, among which were rare specimens of precious stones.

While speaking of Dr. Clarke's library, we should not have omitted to notice his travelling library. It was packed closely, in a case made for the purpose, and comprised the following volumes:—A Greek and Latin Testament, a Septuagint, Hebrew Bible, Pawsham's edition of the English Bible, 1776,—Horace, Virgil, and a small copy of the English Prayer Book. These books were the companions of his frequent excursions to Ireland, the Shetland Islands, and in his tours throughout England.

The question has, perhaps, occurred to our readers while we have been giving this account of the size and value of Dr. Clarke's library and museum, by what means could an individual in his profession obtain such a collection?

The secret of his finding opportunities is, no doubt, in the application of his unequalled industry in this direction, having continued his accumulations for full half a century. The money was obtained by the profits of his publications, although several valuable manuscripts were given away, the profits to be applied to benevolent purposes. Besides all this, his being known as a collector of curious and ancient things and a judge of rare and valuable books, would induce many persons to give him such things as presents.

The frequent preaching of Dr. Clarke must have excited the astonishmeut of our readers, especially when considered in connection with his other labours. From 1782 to 1808, a period of twenty-six years, he preached upon an average, two sermons for every three days. When we remember the several occasions, during these years, of prostrating sickness with which he suffered, the question will be prompted, *how* could it be done? We shall attempt to answer this question, while portraying more fully than we have done, his character as a preacher.

Dr. Clarke possessed a ready utterance, and an exhaustless flow of cheerful feeling, which no degree of toil, nor even the enfeebling influence of old age could destroy, nor much abate. These gave a freshness to his pulpit ministrations which awakened a corresponding feeling in his hearers. While his heart was burning with the message he brought, he could not be at a loss for something to say. This feeling was stimulated, no doubt, by the immense crowds which, from the first to the last day of his public life, waited upon his ministry. These multitudes were both the consequence and the cause of his thought and expression.

The evidence of this popularity is abundant. Having an appointment to preach at Bandon, Ireland, he proceeded thither with some of his friends. "Had a prince entered the town, scarcely greater tokens of respectful recognition could have been shown. Persons were posted all along the street by which the carriages entered from Cork, who had been eagerly awaiting his arrival. Friends and strangers were collected from every part of the circuit, extending thirteen miles, and several had travelled thirty miles to hear the word of life from his lips."

It is said that any chapel of the Wesleyan connection (and some of them accommodated immense multitudes) would be crowded, irrespective of the hour or the weather, on the announcement of his name to preach, though the hour might be five o'clock in the morning, (as was often the case,) and on one of the working days of the week. The record of his death in the conference minutes contains the remark, that "No man, in any age of the church, was ever known, for so long a period, to have attracted larger audiences." But the stimulus of animated feeling, and varied and large audiences, can account, but in a small degree, for his ability of frequent and successful preaching. His constant study of the Word of God was a more important means. All the studies of his life were pursued in reference to the illustration of that Word; and were, therefore, in their influences upon his mind and heart, a constant preparation for the pulpit. Thus, his stores of knowledge brought to his public ministrations, though so multiplied, a surprising variety. He seldom preached from the same text the second time, and when the theme of a former discourse came up, as it often must, it was so varied, and in a relation so new, that the hearers who had listened to it before, had their interest quickened thereby, rather than lessened. This habit of keeping the fountain always full with that food for the heart and mind which had a direct relation to his public office, took the place, to a considerable extent, of immediate preparation. Yet he by no means neglected a specific arrangement of his thoughts before entering the pulpit. In this collecting of his mind he became absorbed. While walking to the house of God, or entering the private room, (always connected with the pulpit in England,) he engaged in no conversation, nor did he seem to be aware of what was passing around him. He never wrote out fully, as a preparation, what he was to preach; but with well arranged ideas, he left the mode of utterance to the warmth of the moment. His manner of handling his subject was rather expository, though not strictly so.

Another source of his pulpit power was a natural strength of mind, to which few could lay claim, and which no study can create—though in genius, as a preacher, he had his superiors in his own day. Yet, in power over the masses, he excelled; or, to use his own expression, "out-congregationed" them all.

But we have not yet given the most important cause of his ability to preach often and to preach well. It was undoubtedly the extraordinary degree of the Holy Spirit's influence with which he was favoured. He lived spiritually near to God, and seemed always to feel "Thou God seest me!" Under this influence he aimed to reach the heart, and to bring men to Christ. His sentiments on this subject, which were exhibited in his practice, he thus expresses:—"The only preaching worth any thing, in God's account, and which the fire will not burn up, is that which labours to convict and convince the sinner of his sin, to bring him into contrition for it, to convert him from it; to lead him to the blood of the covenant, that his conscience may be purged from its guilt,—to the spirit of judgment and burning, that he may be purified from its infection—and then to build him up on this most holy faith, by causing him to pray in the Holy Ghost, and keep himself in the love of God, looking for the mercy of our Lord Jesus Christ unto eternal life. This system is that alone which God will own in the conversion of sinners. I speak from the experience of nearly fifty years in the public ministry of the Word; this is the most likely method to produce the active *soul* of divinity. Labour to bring sinners to God, should you by it bring yourself to the grave."

Dr. Clarke's written sermons differed widely from those which were spoken. The former were prepared in the study, and to be studied. He never carried the show of learning into the pulpit. He dwelt much there on the great fundamental truths respecting which the Christian world generally agree. The depravity of man, the supreme divinity of Christ, his death to save men, and salvation through faith in his blood alone, were his favourite themes. While his thoughts were rich, and gratified the learned and intellectual, they were expressed with so much simplicity of language and cordiality of feeling, that they edified and delighted the most illiterate and feeble disciple. An old lady in the Shetland Isles remarked:—"I had heard that Dr. Clarke was a great man, and very learned; but when I heard him, I found him just like any other man. I could understand every word he said." His voice was clear and strong, but not trained by the arts of the elocutionist—his gestures few and not remarkably expressive. He had the appearance in the pulpit of one having something to say, and a heart which burned with it, and it found expression in the voice and manner, in the readiest and most natural way.

We need not add any illustrations of Dr. Clarke's moral integrity and genuine piety. If the facts of these pages teach any thing, they teach that he was ready to maintain his integrity with a martyr's faithfulness, and that he maintained his piety by an humble faith.

In speaking of his love for friends, he says: "God has given me a body and a mind that have gone through a great deal;—I can live sparingly—do with little raiment—with little sleep, and very little food, but there is one thing I never have been able to live without,—MY FRIENDS. Next to God himself, I must have these or I could not live."

But in no way, perhaps, was his habitual kindness more manifest than when surrounded with a group of frolicking children. With a natural dignity which won respect, and a playfulness that secured their sympathy and love, he made himself exceedingly popular with the little folks. He would form a semicircle of them about the fire in the evening, and relate some Eastern tale, or incident in his own eventful life—and no one could better tell a story, whether to old or young people—always drawing from it such instruction, as to profit as well as amuse. With the girls he would enter into their interest in a doll, and with the boys, into theirs in a game of cricket, as happily as any of them.

The following letter to his grandson breathes the same spirit:—

My Dear Little Grandson,—

Your father and mother tell me you are fond of birds, especially pretty little birds, that have pretty feathers—blue, green, yellow, red, fine glossy black, and fair lily white, with nice bills and beautiful legs; but your mamma tells me that you have but one such bird; what a pity, when you love it so well, and would take great care of others also, if you had them. Well, my dear Adam, I have many very beautiful birds which have been sent me from countries very far off, and they were sent me by very good people who love me, and I will give some of them to you, Adam, because I love you. Now, my dear Adam, I much like these little birds. Is it because they have very beautiful feathers, and beaks, and legs? or because, when they were alive, they sang so delightfully, ran so fast, and flew so swiftly? All this indeed I love, but I love them most because it was the same good God who made them that made myself; and he who feeds me, feeds them also, and takes care of them; and he made them beautiful, that you and I and all people, might be pleased with their fine feathers and sweet singing. Now, a man who has a great deal of money may go to a place where people sing for money; or have music in the house, such as your dear Cecilia plays; but there are a great many poor people in the world who have scarcely money enough to buy bread when they are hungry, or clothes to keep them warm in the cold weather. Now, my dear, these cannot hire people to sing, nor can they have music in their houses, like your mamma, yet they love to hear music; so would it not be a pity that they should not have some also? See, then, why the good God who made you, formed so many fine birds, with such sweet voices to sing the sweetest songs; these are *the poor man's music*, they sing to him for nothing! They do not even ask a crumb of bread from the poor man; and when he is going to work in the morning, they sing to encourage him; and when he is returning home in the evening very weary, because he has worked very hard, they sing again that he may be pleased and not grieve nor fret. Now, is not God very good for making these pretty little musicians to encourage and comfort the poor labouring man? And will you not then love this God who made them for so kind a purpose?

Now you must know, Adam, that I am very fond of these nice little birds; and often take crumbs of bread and scatter them under the windows, that they may come and pick them up; and I once put a stick in the ground before the parlour window, with a cross stick upon the top of it, just like your letter T that you have been learning in your A, B, C, and often would I lift up the window and cry, "Bobby, Bobby," and the sweet redbreast, so soon as he could hear my voice, would fly near the window and sit on the cross stick; and then I left the crumbs and bits of cheese, of which they are very fond, upon the ledge of the window, and when I had shut down the sash, then Bobby would come and eat them all up! I have told you before, that I love little birds; yes, I love them even when they are dead; and I get their skins stuffed, and made to look just as if the birds were alive. Now I send you several of these beautiful stuffed birds, and they shall be your own, and you shall take care of them, and keep them for the sake of your loving and affectionate grandfather,

ADAM CLARKE.

In considering the secret of the success of a man who has accomplished much for the good of his fellow man, it is not easy to designate any one element in his character. There is generally a combination of many. But still, one trait may stand forth more prominently than the rest, and be more easily connected with his success. The INDUSTRY of Dr. Clarke was such a trait. If this was not the whole cause of his greatness and usefulness, without it, he would not have been distinguished. There was a natural strength of mind,—a marked ability—which prompted his unremitted application; but this again was cultivated with a diligence, which all can imitate, that roused and expanded every faculty with which he was gifted. His industry astonished his contemporaries and drew from them frequent expressions of surprise. The influence of his example and precepts in this respect, was felt by all he associated with. An indolent person could not long be his companion, nor endure his society. An economist of time himself, he could not bear to see it wasted by others; and even when his little grandchildren were around him for a time, he always kept them engaged according to their ability. To one he would give a book of pictures to look over,—to another different bits of coloured stones, or paper, to arrange on the floor,—to a third a piece of board with a hammer and nails, to drive in and pull out again; in order that even their infancy should not know the evils of idleness."

A necessary part of his industry was his promptness in the discharge of duty. He answered letters as soon as they were received; and in this way wrote, on an average, during one of the years of his presidency in the Conference, an *official* letter every day, besides an extensive general correspondence.

He says, "I never lost a coach or a boat in my life, by being behind the time of their departure." Railroads of more recent days, would have tried his punctuality still more, but yet we think he would not have "missed the cars."

A catalogue of books having been sent to him late one evening, he immediately looked it over, and saw advertised a rare and valuable book. Early the next morning he was at the book-store, and secured the prize. A few moments after a distinguished literary friend called for the same purpose, but the book was gone. Taking Dr. Clarke's residence in his way on his return, he called for a sight of the work.

"Ah, Doctor," he exclaimed, "you have been fortunate; but how did you secure it? I was at the book-store directly after breakfast."

"But I was there *before* breakfast," replied Dr. Clarke.

A habit of doing every thing in an orderly manner was an attendant of Dr. Clarke's industry. An intimate friend of his, having just left the study, was about to sit down at the breakfast-table.

"You are wanted in my study," said the doctor.

The person immediately proceeded to the study, looked around, but seeing no one, returned, saying, "Who wants me, sir? I find no one there."

"Did you not see a book on the library table, which insisted on again being put in its proper place?" replied the doctor, so good-naturedly that no offence was given, while the lesson on order was not likely to be forgotten.

Early rising being a subject of conversation with a young friend, the latter remarked that he found it impossible to convert the practice of very early rising into that source of enjoyment which it seemed to be to the doctor; that he had been protesting and praying against it for several years, but it still lingered, and seemed to be an inveterate evil.

"My dear brother," said the doctor, "you have entirely misapprehended the case. The remedy is simple, and of easy application. Now, instead of lying in bed and praying on the subject of early rising, I get up at the appointed time, dress myself, and go at once to my study and my books. If you take my advice, you will act, in future, on the same maxim."

Thus industry,—combined with its relative habits of order, promptness, and early rising,—was an important secret, if not the great cause of Dr. Clarke's distinction. This is not only imitable, but it will be as valuable to any of our young readers, as it was to Dr. Clarke. Not that they may accomplish as much as he did, but their ability may be as much quickened and enlarged by it. We may desire his fair fame. Are we willing to pay the price he paid?

CHAPTER XIX.

THE CLOSING SCENE.

The testimony of Dr. Clarke's last years—The seasons of his life—Continued love for the Bible—Recollections—He did not hope to be saved by what he had done—The testimony of the poet Montgomery—Dr. Clarke at the Wesleyan Conference—Leaves for home on account of the prevalence of the cholera—Settles his business—His last attendance at the family altar—His last interview with his children and grandchildren—Parting moments at Hayden Hall—Attacked by cholera—The closing scene.

IT is customary to give the *dying* experience of Christians, in confirmation of the excellence of our holy religion. This is well. But if we give Dr. Clarke's views, while yet in health, of the service of Christ, though standing knowingly on the very verge of the grave, it will be a testimony scarcely less solemn and weighty. He was now old, and his life had been given, from youth to hoary age, to God. Little was left but the solemn opening of eternal scenes. How did that life appear to him in the retrospect, and that eternity now so near? We preface the account of his death with a few declarations on this point, from his own lips.

Dr. Clarke was visiting Port Stuart, and

viewing the shore near which he was so nearly drowned. Turning from contemplating the great deep, he cut out, on a pane of glass, with the point of a diamond, in a careful hand, the following lines:

"THE SEASONS OF ADAM CLARKE S LIFE.

"I have enjoyed the *spring of life*,—
I have endured the *toils* of its *summer*—
I have *culled* the fruits of its *autumn*—
I am now passing through the rigours of its *winter*—
And I am neither forsaken of GOD
Nor abandoned of *man*.
I see, at no great distance, the *dawn* of a *new day*,
The first of a *spring* that shall be eternal!
It is advancing to meet me!
I run to embrace it!
Welcome! welcome! *eternal* spring!
Hallelujah!"

We have, in the following records, his last testimony concerning the excellence of the *Bible*, over which so many days of study and toil had been spent.

"*In perpetuam rei memoriam.** I have lived more than three-score years and ten. I have travelled a good deal, by sea and land. I have conversed with, and seen many people, in, and from many different countries. I have studied all the principal religious systems in the world. I have read much, thought much, and rea-

* "For a perpetual memorial."

soned much; and the result is, I am persuaded of the simple, unadulterated truth of no book but of the Bible, and of the excellence of no system of religion but that contained in the Holy Scriptures; and especially, Christianity, which is referred to in the Old Testament, and fully revealed in the New." He expresses himself in the same spirit in a letter to a young friend:

"After having, for more than half a century, read the Bible so much, I formed the resolution in January, 1830, to read the Bible through once more, beginning with the first chapter of Genesis, and the first of Matthew, binding myself to read a chapter of each every day. I read the New Testament in Greek, and the Old Testament in English, comparing it, occasionally, with the Hebrew. I bind myself to one chapter in each, daily; but I often read more, and have, since the first of last January, read over the five books of Moses and the four Gospels. This I find very profitable.

At the close of the year he speaks of the results of this resolution. The Greek I read alone, and every word aloud, to accustom myself to speak it regularly and correctly—for the facility of speaking either it or any other language would be soon lost without this. I thought it might be the last year I might be permitted to go through again with the Book of God; and if so, I would take my leave of it in full. Some days I read two chapters in the

Old Testament and one in the New. On other days I could not do so much; but there were some in which I could do much more, and read four or five. This got me a little before-hand, when I had to travel. At the conference I was a little back; but as I rose early, I accomplished the whole in the course of the year, in the midst of travelling, preaching, writing, and other employment.

During his last journey to Ireland in behalf of his schools, being in indifferent health, and weary from incessant travelling and preaching, he thus expresses his feelings:—

"My youthful days were spent in labour; my manhood in hard and incessant toil; and now my old age is consuming fast away in travail and care; and when care is unavoidably crowned by anxiety, the taper of life must soon sink in its socket. An active mind will ever say, 'Better wear out than rust out;' but there is a difference between *wear* out and *grind* out. The one implies regular, though continual labour; the other extra employment, and violent exercise. When I look back upon my three-score and ten years, I must say, I find little *wearing*. All has been *grinding* with me. Strong attrition has acted on every part, and my candle has been lighted at both ends. Under the blessing of God, I have been the former of my own fortune. I have never been importunate for wealth or favour.

I have not been troublesome to any. I have not eaten my bread for nought, nor have I eaten my morsel alone. Often have the necessities of others fallen upon me, and strangely has God supported me under them. The Lord knoweth the way that I take, and when he hath tried me I shall come forth as gold; only speak thou the word, and thy servant heareth."

At another time, after noticing several particulars connected with his personal history as a Christian, and the accessions which had been made to his literary stores, he said, "If I had the offer of millions of money, on condition that the knowledge of these things, their associations, and the feelings excited by them, should, in the recollection, be as though they were not, I would at once say, take your millions, and preserve to me this knowledge. If I had it in my power to change any of the scenes and associations through which I have passed, I would not alter one iota that has come in this way."

Though he thus speaks of *himself*, the following declaration to a friend,—almost a *dying* testimony,—will show with what he connected all the good he had been enabled to do:—

"My record is with God, who knows as well my sincerity and uprightness, as he knows my worthlessness and weakness,—nor have I ever sought to balance these in order to have the cold consolation, 'I stand, if not in the list of merit, yet among the blameless.' No. I said to my God, 'Thou knowest the way that I take; I have endeavoured to promote thy glory by striving to do good to thy creatures redeemed by the blood of thy Son; but, in these respects, I cannot stand with uncovered face before thee; and thou knowest that my heart says more forcibly than my voice can say, 'God be mericiful to me, a sinner.'

"God never needed my services. He brought me into the world that I might receive good from him and do good to my fellows. This is God's object in reference to all human beings, and should be the object of every man in reference to his brother. This is the whole of my practical creed. God, in his love, gave me a being; in his mercy he has done every thing he should do to make it a well-being. He has taught me to love him by first loving me; and has taught me to love my neighbours as myself, by inspiring me with his own love."

"O thou incomprehensible Jehovah, thou eternal Word, the ever-enduring and all pervading Spirit—Father, Son, and Holy Ghost! in the plenitude of thy eternal Godhead, in thy light, I, in a measure, see Thee; and in thy condescending nearness to my nature, I can love Thee for Thou hast loved me. In thy strength may I begin, continue and end every design, and every work, so as to glorify Thee, by showing how much thou lovest man, and how much man may be ennobled by loving Thee!"

We shall close these notices of Dr. Clarke's religious feeling, in his last years, by the testimony of another, who witnessed one of his last public labours, a few weeks only before his death—the testimony of one, not of his own branch of Christ's church, but extensively known where Christian poetry is loved—the late James Montgomery. The words which follow were spoken by him in a public meeting in Sheffield, in reference to Dr. Clarke's last ministrations there:

"Few probably are here now, who will not call to mind one who was among us, on a like occasion, last year—one who, by his sermons from the pulpit on the Sabbath, his address at the public meeting on the Monday, and his farewell to the breakfast party next morning, most effectually served the cause which he was engaged to plead, by making those who had the privilege of hearing him, determine to render their own services more effective thenceforward; witnessing, as they did, the zeal, faith and love of that venerable disciple towards the close of his career."

"Who among us does not remember—nay, which of us can forget—the two discourses referred to? the simple energy with which they were poured forth, the unction of the Holy One which accompanied them, and the devout feeling so interfused as to overpower the sense of admiration which the learning, the love, the transcendent ability displayed in the composition, were calculated to excite. Then his address to the meeting from this platform, though uttered under the pressure of great bodily weakness, was hallowed throughout by such demonstration of the Spirit and of power, as to leave an imperishable recollection of its influence upon our minds; while, with patriarchal grace, he told the simple tale of his own early experience of the gospel, and showed how it constrained him to sally forth, boy as he was, among the mountains and valleys, to the hamlets and scattered huts, in the wild neighbourhood where he was born, with New Testament and hymn book in hand, preaching and praying, reading and singing, wherever he could collect a few peasants, or women and children about him to hearken to his voice, or join with him in worship. The scene, too, after the breakfast, in the adjacent vestry, was most touching and impressive. He knew not how to give over, while from the fulness of his heart, his mouth spake. His last words—of which more and more fell from his lips as he lingered in the room, and could not depart without again and again exhorting the company to diligence and fidelity to the service of God—those last words left a blessing behind which can never be taken away from those on whom it descended; even as Elijah, before he was carried up to heaven in the chariot of fire already waiting for him, may be supposed to have turned back and spread abroad his hands in benediction towards the sons of the prophets who tarried on the other side of Jordan, while he on whom his mantle was to fall, accompanied him to the farther side. Such was Adam Clarke when we last beheld him."

Our biographical narrative is now closed. There remains only the sad duty of relating how the venerable servant of God passed the Jordan of death.

Though in feeble health, he attended the Wesleyan Conference, in Liverpool, the latter part of July, 1832. Strong expressions of Christian love and confidence passed between him and his brethren in the ministry. He occupied the chair of the president during his temporary absence, and preached the annual sermon before the conference at the repeated unanimous vote of that body. Thus having taken, unconsciously, his last leave of his brethren in the ministry of the Word, he hastened away, before the close of the sittings of the conference, assigning as a reason, not only his own health, but the desire he had to be with his family during the prevalence of the cholera, which was then making fearful ravages around him. "God," said he, "is visiting this nation, he is visiting this town, which has become a place of death; he has long had a reckoning with us as a land; we are in the midst of disease; it is in the metropolis; my house will be filled with children—there is no barricading the house against the scourge—I must go and be with them."

Just before his departure for home, while in the house of a friend, the cholera being the subject of conversation, it was remarked, by a person present, that the wife of one of the preachers had suffered much from fear of the cholera, but was delivered from that fear by the application of the following text of Scripture to her, which she received as a revelation from God, that she should not be touched by the cholera—"A thousand shall fall at thy side and ten thousand at thy right hand; but it shall not come nigh thee," &c. Ps. xci. The doctor rebuked this interpretation by saying, "Mrs. H. may have such an impression, and she may believe she has been told so, but this I know, that God has not so spoken to me."

Deeply convinced that he might at any moment be called from his connection with the church on earth, he had, before leaving the conference, transferred all his responsibilities for the Shetland Mission to them, and made arrangements to confide to the same care his Irish schools, which had until now been in their management, on his sole responsibility. His monied accounts were all brought into the most exact order, with as much promptness as if he knew he was about to retire from earthly scenes.

On the 21st of August, the doctor arrived at Haydon Hall. In his morning and evening worship with his family, he invariably prayed, in reference to the cholera, that each and all might be preserved from its influence or prepared for sudden death. On Saturday, August 25th, he summoned his family as usual, for morning devotions. He commenced with these words, "We thank thee, O heavenly Father, that we have a blessed hope through Christ of entering into thy glory." Having an engagement at Bayswater, to preach on Sabbath morning, his friend, Mr. Hobbs, of that place, came with a carriage to carry him to his house for the night. Dr. Clarke had, but four days before, visited all his children, kissed most affectionately his grand-children, and literally blessed, as was his custom, in the name of God, his own children and theirs. On stepping into the carriage, he gave a piece of silver to a servant, for "poor Mrs. Fox," a sick and now dying neighbour, whose sufferings his charity and attention had for a long time alleviated, inquiring at the same after her spiritual welfare. When told that she was peacefully trusting in Christ, he exclaimed.

"Praise God," and left his own gate—forever. Could a farewell have been more fitting, had it been known to be such!

On his arrival at Bayswater, he was much fatigued, and spoke but little. He retired early. About six o'clock the next morning he came down and requested the servant to call Mr. Hobbs. He found Dr. Clarke standing with his great coat on, and ready for a journey. Addressing Mr. Hobbs, he said, "My dear fellow, you must get me home directly; without a miracle I could not preach; get me home—I want to be home." It was soon found necessary to call for a physician, who pronounced the disease to be the cholera. When Mrs. Clarke entered the room, about four in the afternoon, he was only able to extend his hand towards her; and, on the appearance of Mrs. Hook, one of his daughters, he opened his eyes and strove to clasp his fingers upon her hand. The disease baffled all human skill; and, at twenty minutes before eleven o'clock, in the stillness of a Sabbath night, in the seventy-second year of his age, Adam Clarke fell "asleep in Jesus."

The text from which he had proposed to preach that Sabbath was legibly written upon some paper which was left upon his table at home; he had evidently intended to write out his thoughts upon it for preservation. It was this—"Verily, verily I say unto you, the hour is coming and now is, when the dead shall hear the voice of the Son of God; and they that hear shall live." John x. In the burying-ground, behind the Wesleyan Chapel, City Road, London, in an humble grave, next to the vault in which repose the ashes of the venerable John Wesley, all that was mortal of Adam Clarke lies buried.

"Servant of God, well done!
Thy glorious warfare's past;
The battle's fought, the race is won,
And thou art crowned at last."

www.ingramcontent.com/pod-product-compliance
Lightning Source LLC
LaVergne TN
LVHW050521100826
845148LV00002B/404

* 9 7 8 1 4 2 5 5 2 0 9 1 5 *